# The UK Economy 2003-2013

**Nick Fyfe**
*Head of Economics, Dulwich College*

**Andrew Threadgold**
*Staff Tutor, Dulwich College*

**informe**

**Acknowledgements and thanks**

Many thanks to Peter Maunder for all his efforts and expertise as editor
and advisor, and to Ian Black for his work on previous editions.

Anforme Ltd, Stocksfield Hall, Stocksfield, Northumberland NE43 7TN.

Typeset by George Wishart & Associates, Whitley Bay.
Printed by Potts Print (UK) Ltd.

# Contents

# Chapter 1

# GDP: Boom, Bust and Recovery

## Introduction

The UK economic story between 2003 and 2013 is a story of growth: initially, strong and positive; latterly, the quest for growth as the economy struggled to recover from two quick-fire recessions has become somewhat desperate. This chapter will set out key events, necessarily drawing on wider economic variables and serving as an introduction to the content of later sections. In addition, it is also important to note that economic performance during this period is best understood within the context of what has gone before. There will be a strong emphasis on the period 2003-2013, but data and events from the 1990s and even the 1980s are necessary for a full understanding of the trends and pressures in the UK macroeconomy.

Having noted the growth performance of the UK economy since 1990 we examine the movement of the components of GDP. We show the changes in the base rate of interest, the unemployment rate, rate of price inflation and stock market indices to reveal the unstable nature of the UK economy during the past two decades.

## ● Knowledge: **Economic growth**

Economic growth – the increase in the productive capacity in an economy – is a fundamental measure of macroeconomic performance. The trend rate of economic growth for the UK economy has been assumed for several years to be between 2.5% and 2.75% per year. This implies that the total output of the economy, if all factors of production (land, labour, capital, enterprise) were fully utilised, would grow by this percentage each year.

However measuring productive capacity is very difficult, and thus economists focus on the more accessible measure of economic growth as the percentage change in Gross Domestic Product (GDP). GDP measures actual output: the total value of output in the whole economy over a given period of time.

## ● Application: **A brief history of UK growth**

*Figure 1.1: UK real GDP growth*

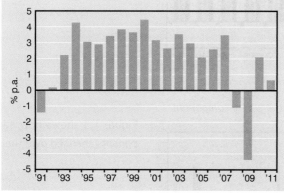

Source: HM Treasury

As Figure 1.1 shows, the actual growth rate of the UK economy has fluctuated significantly from year to year.

A **recession** occurs where real GDP growth is negative for at least two consecutive quarters. Over the period shown in Figure 1.1 the UK economy experienced two recessions: in the early 1990s and in 2008-2009. In addition, the UK economy re-entered recession in quarter 4 of 2011 and the first quarter of 2012 as real GDP shrank again. A **boom** is a period during which real GDP rises at a faster rate than assumed growth in productive capacity. The long boom of 1997-2007 can clearly be seen on Figure 1.1.

**Recovery**, or upturn, often marks the period between the end of a recession and the beginning of a boom. During this stage of the economic cycle, real GDP is positive, rising, but still below the long-run growth rate. On the other hand, a slowdown or downturn occurs when real GDP growth is positive but falling and is below the long-run growth rate.

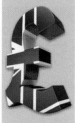

## Question

1. Using Figure 1.1, give examples of each of the following: boom, slowdown, recession, recovery.

Macroeconomic policies tend to focus on creating stable and sustainable economic growth. **Supply-side policies** aim to increase the long-run average, or trend level of growth which shows increases in productive capacity. This will be explored in greater detail in Chapter 6 when we examine productivity and competitiveness in greater detail. **Demand-management policies** such as fiscal and monetary measures are used to control actual GDP and take a shorter-term approach to macroeconomic stability. These policies are explored in greater depth in Chapters 9 and 10 respectively.

When investigating the story of the UK in recent years, economic growth is a key indicator of the health and potential of the UK macroeconomy.

● ● **Application and Analysis: Components of UK GDP**

GDP measures the total value of output, expenditure and incomes across the economy over a given period of time. Macroeconomists break down GDP into four key areas:

**Consumption (C)**          Spending by households on consumer goods e.g. food, holidays, clothes

**Investment (I)**          Spending by firms on capital goods e.g. machinery, vehicles, plant

**Government Spending (G)**          Spending by the public sector e.g. infrastructure, public sector wages, NHS costs

**Net Exports (X-M)**          Spending by foreigners on UK goods minus spending by the UK on foreign goods

*Figure 1.2: UK GDP by component*

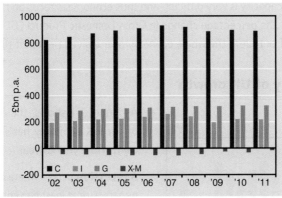

Source: HM Treasury

Figure 1.2 shows the importance of consumer spending for the UK economy over the period shown. The effect of the recession in 2008-09 can be seen on both consumption and investment, along with the fall in net exports resulting from recession in the UK's main trading partners.

*Figure 1.3: Economic growth in the UK by component*

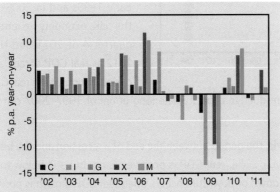

Source: HM Treasury

Figure 1.3 shows how each of these components changed over the same period.

● Analysis: **Explaining fluctuations in real GDP growth**

*Figure 1.4: UK business confidence in the service and manufacturing sector*

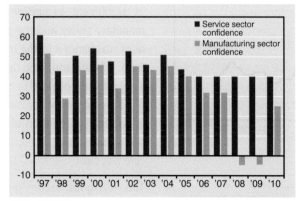

Source: HM Treasury

*Figure 1.5: UK consumer confidence*

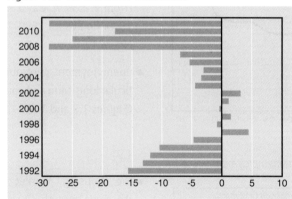

Source: HM Treasury

**1991-1997: Recession and export-led growth**

The UK experienced recession in the early 1990s. Stock markets crashed in 1987 in the USA and across Europe. The UK economy continued to grow until 1990 but as oil prices were pushed higher by the Gulf War, both consumer price inflation and the base rate reached double figures. Falling real incomes and the negative wealth effect from a struggling housing market pushed the UK into its deepest recession since the Second World War. In September 1992 the domestic currency, sterling, was forced out of the Exchange Rate Mechanism, which was the system used to ensure national currencies converged in preparation for the creation of the single European currency, the euro.

The period 1992-1997 saw recovery from recession. The weaker value of sterling helped to boost exports, particularly to other European countries, and although business and consumer confidence was not always high (the UK housing market was flat over this period, for example) there were signs of growth in the service sector and the UK economy began to emerge as a modern, service-based consumer economy.

*Spending by households on consumer goods such as clothes is the most important element of UK GDP.*

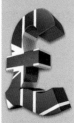

Figure 1.6: UK base rate of interest

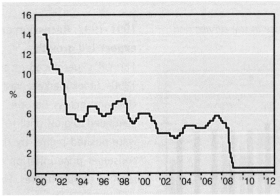

Source: Bank of England

Figure 1.7: UK unemployment

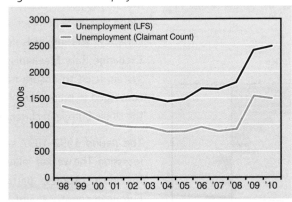

Source: HM Treasury

Figure 1.8: Long-term and youth unemployment in the UK

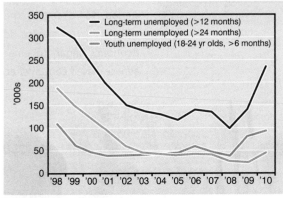

Source: HM Treasury

Figure 1.9: UK inflation, Consumer Price Index

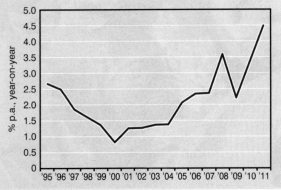

Source: HM Treasury

## 1997-2000: Early days of New Labour

With a New Labour government in place with an emphasis on growth and economic stability, the UK economy began a period of significant expansion. The control of monetary policy and the setting of interest rates was handed to the newly-independent Bank of England, and although the new administration pledged to maintain Conservative spending plans for their first three years in power, the intention of significant public sector investment in education and healthcare was clear.

The 'feel good factor' returned to the UK economy:

● interest rates fell through 1998 and 1999 (from 7.25% in May 1998 to 5% by June 1999; figures for 1990-2012 are shown on Figure 1.6)

● unemployment continued to fall, in particular long-term and youth unemployment (Figures 1.7 and 1.8)

● low and falling inflationary pressure (Figure 1.9)

● the housing market experienced its strongest growth since the early 1990s, increasing household wealth through positive equity for homeowners (Figure 1.10)

● strong stock market performance, increasing household wealth for shareholders (Figure 1.11)

These factors combined to boost consumption and investment, and confidence also grew in expectation of an extensive programme of public sector investment.

Figure 1.10: UK housing market indicators

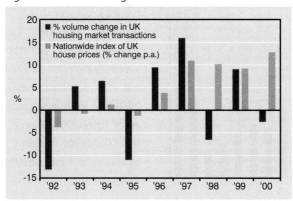

Source: HM Treasury

Figure 1.11: FTSE All Share Index

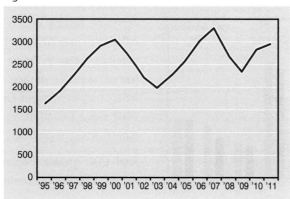

Source: HM Treasury

Figure 1.12: NASDAQ Composite Index

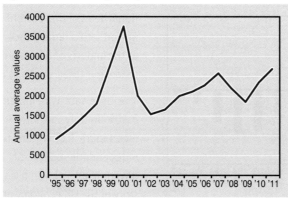

Source: HM Treasury

Figure 1.13: Annual change in selected stock market indices

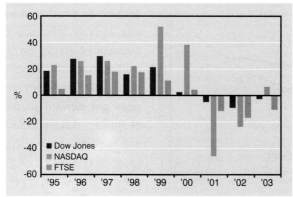

Source: HM Treasury

## 2000-2003: Turbulent times

By the turn of the millennium, it was clear the 'mini-boom' of 1997-2000 was coming to an end. The FTSE index increased by less than 5% over 2000 compared to double-digit growth in 1996-99 (see Figure 1.11). Even before the terrorist attacks in New York in September 2001, the US economy had faltered as the dot-com boom (and associated economic expansion created by the growth of new technology spending and investment) came to an end.

On March 10, 2000 the NASDAQ (the second-largest stock exchange in the USA, which pioneered online trading and was the exchange of choice for the new technology firms associated with the internet boom of 1995-2000) Composite index reached its peak of 5.132.52. Figure 1.12 shows the average annual values of this index between 1995 and 2011.

Over the course of 2011, the NASDAQ lost almost half of its value, with significant losses also recorded on the Dow Jones and FTSE indices (Figure 1.13).

These problems in the US economy were compounded by the tragic events in New York on the 9th September 2001, and the economic impact in the UK was one of shaken confidence and fears for future growth. The saving ratio for UK households, which had fallen steadily since the early 1990s (see Figure 1.14), recorded a small increase in 2001, and house price growth dipped in 2000 and 2001, albeit still increasing above the rate of inflation (housing market transactions also continued to rise as shown in Figure 1.15).

*Figure 1.14: UK saving ratio*

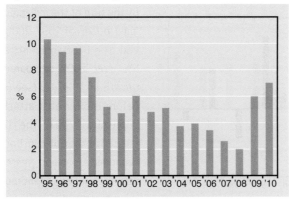

Source: HM Treasury

*Figure 1.15: UK housing market inflation*

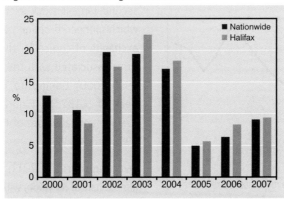

Source: HM Treasury

*Figure 1.16: UK budget position at constant 2010-11 prices*

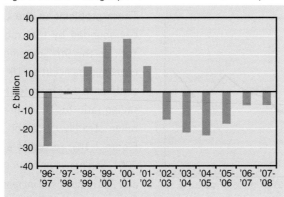

Source: HM Treasury

*Figure 1.17: UK economic data*

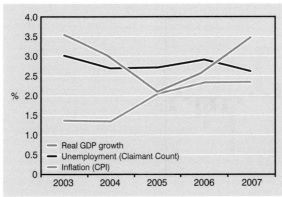

Source: HM Treasury

The period 2000 to 2003 also marked a shift towards greater fiscal injection into the economy. The New Labour government elected in 1997 had stuck to Conservative spending plans for its first two years in office, but after a second election victory in May 2001 the budget surpluses built up in the years 1998-2001 (Figure 1.16) were viewed by Chancellor Gordon Brown as being available to fund significant public sector investment.

### 2003-2007: Steady, stable growth

The story of the most recent decade of UK economic history begins with house price inflation of over 20% according to the Halifax index as shown in Figure 1.15. The second half of 'the NICE decade' (a period of Non-Inflationary Continuous Expansion) of 1997-2007 was a period of recovering economic growth after the problems of 2000-2001.

Real GDP growth began and ended this period above its trend rate of 2.5%, unemployment fell and inflation was under control. This stability allowed business and consumer confidence to recover in the UK; nonetheless, the current account position moved into a large deficit, most significantly as the imports of goods grew far more quickly than exports, as shown in Figure 1.18.

The base rate was increased steadily from 3.50% in July 2003 to 5.75% in July 2007 (see Figure 1.6). Interest rates – a flagship independent policy of the New Labour government – played a significant role in the story of the UK economy at that time. Interest rate changes influence the wider economy by influencing the consumer and business decision on whether to spend or save; they also directly influence the value of the domestic currency in foreign exchange markets through effects on the patterns of global saving and investment. Higher interest rates put upward pressure on the value of sterling, making exports more expensive and imports cheaper. However, consumer spending remained strong due to a structural movement towards lower saving across the economy. Despite higher consumption and

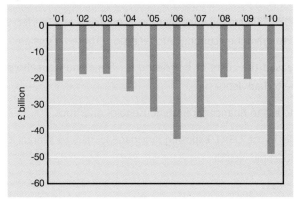

Figure 1.18: UK current account position

Source: HM Treasury

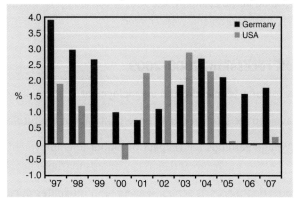

Figure 1.19: UK interest rate (LIBOR) differential with interest rates in Germany and USA (UK minus foreign rate)

Source: HM Treasury

the added injection of a heavy public sector investment programme, inflation remained low, suppressed by falling import prices and the powerful force of globalisation. Thus UK interest rates were a dangerous combination of *historically low* but nevertheless *relatively high* compared with interest rates elsewhere. Figure 1.6 showed earlier in this chapter how the base rate was significantly higher in the early 1990s than a decade later. Figure 1.19 compares UK interest rates with those of Germany and the USA during the NICE decade. The differential in the UK interest rate with Germany was 1.5% or more in all but three years, and of the same size as compared with the USA in all but five years.

## Question

2. Using the ideas from this chapter so far, identify the factors which might contribute to strong economic growth in an economy.

### 2007-2013: Recession, recovery, relapse?

Despite the false alarms of 2000-01, UK economic growth and related consumer indicators (most notably the housing market and stock exchange) recovered strongly up to the summer of 2007, when it became obvious that the longest period of positive economic growth since World War Two was coming to an end. The US housing market had peaked in early 2006, fuelled in part by the subprime lending market where banks were willing to issue mortgages to householders previously deemed too risky to lend to. As borrowers defaulted on loans, banks were forced to absorb these losses and in many cases required assistance from

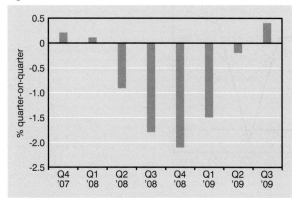

Figure 1.20: UK GDP – the recession of 2008-09

Source: HM Treasury

national governments to remain in business. Business and consumer confidence collapsed (see Figures 1.4 and 1.5) and public sector finances, already under strain as unemployment began to rise, had to be diverted to support financial institutions and avert a total collapse in the banking sector.

After 63 quarters of positive economic growth the UK economy entered recession, recording negative growth in the second quarter of 2008 of -1.3%. Growth remained negative until the third quarter of 2009 (see Figure 1.20).

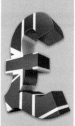

## Analysis: Causes of the UK recession, 2008-2009

The economic conditions of 2007-2009 are regarded by some economists as a 'perfect storm': a combination of factors which combined to drive the economy into recession. These factors are:

- a financial crisis which increased the costs of borrowing for firms and households as banks feared collapse due to their exposure to bad debts

- a subsequent tightening of access to finance for both households and firms

- falling house prices (especially in the USA), exposing mortgage lenders to serious losses and reducing consumer confidence and household wealth

- significant losses on stock markets

- high levels of household debt due to cheap, easy finance and a falling saving ratio in the NICE decade

- rising oil prices (an increase from $55 to $147 barrel between early 2007 and July 2008)

As aggregate demand (total spending in the economy; the sum of consumption, investment, government expenditure and net exports) fell, further problems were created.

## Analysis: Impacts of the UK recession, 2008-2009

- rising joblessness, particularly for long-term and youth unemployment

- fewer job vacancies as firms avoided recruitment due to uncertainty about the future

- falling living standards as average earnings fell (impact of higher unemployment bringing average earnings down, as well as pay freezes and below-inflation pay awards for those people still in work)

- higher demand for higher education places as school-leavers (and graduates pursuing postgraduate courses) sought to remain in education

- a fall in inflation on the RPI measure (Figure 1.21); the differences between CPI and RPI and therefore the explanation for the significant disparity between these measures in 2009 are given in Chapter 8

- a depreciation in sterling (see Chapter 5)

- pressure on the government's budget position, as tax revenues fell (due to downward pressure on incomes, spending and wealth) and spending increased (due to the automatic stabiliser of more unemployment benefit claimants)

*Figure 1.21: RPI and CPI in UK*

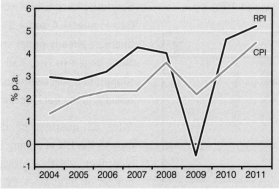

Source: HM Treasury

## ● Analysis: **Anti-recession policies**

The key policy instruments available to governments to control the level of aggregate demand in the economy are monetary and fiscal measures.

**Monetary policy** (This is discussed in detail in Chapter 9):

● drastic cuts in the base rate of interest (see Figure 1.6) culminating in a historically unprecedented base rate of 0.50% from March 2009

● a programme of quantitative easing beginning in March 2009: the purchase of government debt by the Bank of England (by February 2012, the Bank had authorised purchases of up to £325 bn)

● acceptance of a fall in the value of sterling, reducing the price of UK goods in international markets and stimulating export performance

**Fiscal policy** (This is discussed in detail in Chapter 10):

● cuts in tax rates, such as the temporary reduction in VAT from 17.5% to 15% in December 2008

● increases in other taxes, such as the introduction of a top rate of income tax of 50% on earnings over £150,000 per annum and a reduction of tax relief on pensions for high earners

● higher government spending on initiatives such as an extra £1.7bn on the job centre network, to support job seekers, and to help businesses during difficult trading conditions

---

### Question

3. Which policies are likely to be most effective in reducing the severity of a recession?

---

## ● Evaluation: **Is the UK in good shape for recovery in 2013?**

Economists classify recessions according to the pattern of economic growth.

● 'V' shaped recessions see a fall in economic growth followed by quick recovery and return to growth

● 'U' shaped recessions have a longer period of negative growth before recovery

● 'W' shaped recessions, or 'double-dip' recessions, are characterised by some recovery before the economy slips back into negative growth

● 'L' shaped recessions are the worst scenario: negative growth which persists, possibly for several years. Such a recession is sometimes called a **depression**

*Figure 1.22: UK GDP, recovery and another recession in the UK, 2009-2012*

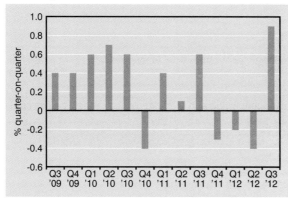

Source: HM Treasury

The experience of the UK since 2009 is shown in Figure 1.22, which extends the data period from Figure 1.20 above.

The UK economy has clearly experienced a double-dip recession. (Note that quarter 4 of 2010 and quarter 1 of 2011 do not count as recessions, as there were not two *consecutive* quarters of negative growth.)

According to a study by the National Institute for Economic and Social Research (NIESR), the economy is not predicted to return to the GDP level experienced at the peak of the previous boom until 2014.

Chancellor George Osborne's Plan A of deficit reduction has not created the stimulus to private sector confidence and growth as he had desired in 2010. The consequences of more negative, or even low positive growth will be very serious for the UK economy, but it is important to remember that even during a time of recession there may be 'winners' as well as 'losers'.

## Question

4. To what extent does the government lack policy options in tackling new fears about economic growth in 2012 and beyond?

## ● Evaluation: Gain and pain in a recession

| 'Winners' in a recession | 'Losers' in a recession |
|---|---|
| **Firms** | |
| ● Lower wage inflation | ● Lower demand, especially for luxury goods |
| ● Larger pool of available workers, some of whom may be highly skilled and desperate to work | ● Negative equity as land and property prices decline |
| ● Higher demand for inferior goods as consumers switch down to less expensive options | ● Possible bankruptcy |
| ● Higher domestic demand if currency depreciates, as exports become more expensive | |
| **Households** | |
| ● Lower borrowing costs and mortgage repayments as base rate is cut | ● Falling real income levels (especially if inflation remains relatively high) |
| ● Lower income tax rates if government uses fiscal policy to stimulate the economy | ● More expensive imports and foreign holidays due to weaker currency |
| ● Cheaper goods and services as firms compete more aggressively for business | ● Threat of unemployment and resulting poverty and hardship |

## Question Extension

5. Why do economies experience an 'economic cycle' where periods of boom are followed by periods of recession?

   Research theories of the economic cycle and evaluate which model is most applicable to the UK economy in 2007-09 and in 2012.

# Chapter 2
# Consumer Spending, Saving and Credit

In this chapter we consider in detail how household expenditure in the UK has moved and discuss the factors which explain differences in the growth rate of this spending.

## ● Knowledge: **Consumption, saving, credit and income**

The concepts of consumer spending, saving and credit are intrinsically linked. **Consumer spending**, also known as **consumption**, is spending by households on goods and services. The most obvious determinant of the consumption level in an economy is **income**. However, households can fund spending from income in different time periods.

- **Past income** – households can draw on **savings** (income previously earned and not consumed) to fund consumption now.

- **Current income** – the most obvious source of funds for consumer spending, but most households will usually try to save some of their income to plan for the future or prepare for contingencies.

- **Future income** – effectively, households can spend future income streams by taking out **credit** and borrowing. Debt repayments will, of course, reduce future consumption levels, and will be influenced by interest rates in credit markets.

To quote John Maynard Keynes, *"the importance of money flows from it being a link between the present and the future."*

## ● Knowledge: **Economic theories of consumption**

The link between income levels and consumption levels is disputed by economists.

### ● Absolute income hypothesis
John Maynard Keynes argued that national income is the key determinant of consumption. Thus when income levels rise, as in a boom, households will spend more money on goods and services. During a recession, consumption will fall. However, the proportion of income used for consumption may differ. Keynes identified the average propensity to consume (APC) and marginal propensity to consume (MPC) as important features of macroeconomics. The Keynesian model also distinguishes between **autonomous consumption** (spending on necessities) and **induced** or **discretionary consumption** (spending on non-essentials). Only discretionary consumption, in this model, is directly related to income.

### ● Life cycle hypothesis
Franco Modigliani argued that households smooth out their spending over their lifetimes. At the beginning of people's careers consumption exceeds income as households take out credit to pay for housing and consumer durables. This is known as **dissaving**, or negative saving. In their middle years, workers pay off debt (e.g. mortgages) and begin to save for old age (positive saving). Later in life, these savings can be used to fund consumption in retirement.

### ● Permanent income hypothesis
Milton Friedman argued that households have a 'permanent income': a rate of return based on ownership of assets (physical assets such as property, and financial assets such as stocks and bonds) and human wealth (skills, education and experience). Short-run shocks, such as redundancy, will not have a major impact on consumption as workers will expect to be re-employed in the future. Only changes to assets and human wealth will affect the permanent income. This is linked to the 'rational expectations' model, where

economic agents take all available information into account and their behaviour is not easily influenced by short-run fluctuations in income or changes in government policy.

### ● Confidence hypothesis

The role of confidence and expectations are important in economics. Both terms imply an opinion or outlook on the future. In periods when consumer confidence is high, households might choose to consume more and save less as a proportion of their income. When confidence is low, households may increase their saving ratio in preparation for possible falls in income.

### ● Relative income hypothesis

James Duesenberry argued that consumer spending is determined by cultural as well as economic factors. Households base spending decisions on previous levels (in particular, past peak income') and in comparison with other households. Thus low income households consume a higher proportion of their income (and save a lower proportion) to maintain a standard of living similar to that of richer households. This theory helps explain why households may continue to spend even when income has fallen drastically, such as during a period of unemployment in a recession or after retirement.

### ● Behavioural models

Recent economic research has examined the psychology of economic decision-making. Behavioural economists are concerned with why economic agents might sometimes behave irrationally, in other words why they make decisions which appear to be less than optimal. Such economists might argue that consumption levels will fluctuate according to the ability of households to defer gratification, which might give important insight into why some people are prone to indebtedness. Other research has suggested that households treat different sources of income in different ways ('mental accounting'). For example, a large 'windfall' income (such as an unexpected bonus or a lottery win) will increase consumption, whereas a small windfall may be saved.

## Question

1. What reasons do each of these models suggest for a less than perfect link between consumer spending and income levels?

## ● ● Application and Analysis: Explaining changes in consumer spending and saving in the UK

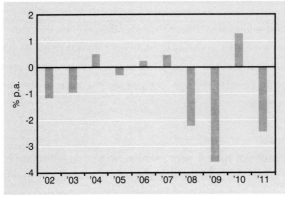

*Figure 2.1: Growth in UK households' consumer spending*

Source: HM Treasury

Figure 2.1 shows the trend in consumer spending growth year on year from 2001 to 2011. Clearly, the impact of recession in 2008 and 2009 and a further loss of confidence in 2011 can be seen on the chart.

*Figure 2.2: Quarterly growth in consumer spending in the UK*

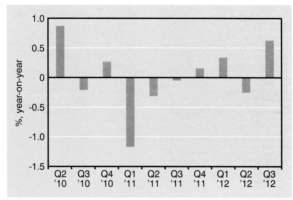

Source: HM Treasury

More recent quarterly data is shown in Figure 2.2. Here, growth is calculated against the equivalent quarter of the previous year, which is known as year-on-year data. This is more useful than quarter-on-quarter growth, which can be distorted by seasonal distributions in spending (for example, Q4, comprising of October, November and December, usually sees a jump in consumer spending due to Christmas).

Clearly, weak recovery and an eventual return to recession can be seen in the decline in consumption growth from as early as the second quarter of 2010. This appears to support the theories which link consumer spending to income levels.

However, what factors explain the high levels of consumption growth up to 2007?

## 1. Rising real disposable incomes

Figure 2.3 shows consumer spending against real GDP since 2002. There is a clear correlation between these two trends, suggesting that national income has a strong influence on household spending.

*Figure 2.3: UK real GDP versus household expenditure*

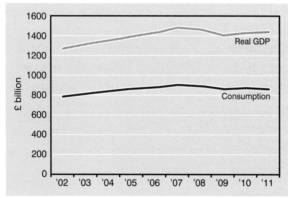

Source: HM Treasury

It should also be noted that consumption growth played a significant role in fuelling the boom (and bust) in the UK economy in recent years. To suggest that higher consumption led to rising national income, which in turn increased consumption, is a circular argument. It is therefore important to consider other factors which have affected both consumer spending and national income in this period.

## 2. Interest rates

Interest rates are a cornerstone of monetary policy (see Chapter 9) and they are used by central banks to influence consumption, investment and export performance. Interest rates affect both the incentive to save and the cost of borrowing, and thus should have a strong impact on household's spending decisions.

Put simply, higher interest rates increase the reward to savers and increase the cost of borrowing. This should increase the saving ratio and reduce consumption on goods more likely to be purchased using credit (housing, and consumer durables such as furniture and cars). Falling interest rates should boost consumer spending by reducing the incentive to save and reducing debt repayments.

The link between the base rate and saving ratio is shown in Figure 2.4. In theory, the data should show a positive correlation, but this is not the case. Even with the base rate at a historic low of 0.5% since 2009, the saving ratio has increased considerably from 3% to over 7% during this period. Also, the general upward trend in the base rate between 2003 and 2007 saw the saving ratio almost halve from 5% to less than 3%.

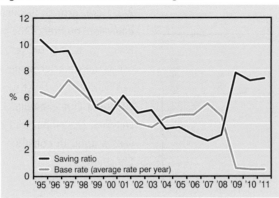

*Figure 2.4: UK base rate and saving ratio*

Source: HM Treasury

One analysis of the period 2003 to 2007 is that interest rates were relatively high but historically low (see Figure 1.19 in Chapter 1). The impact of interest rates on other macroeconomic variables needs to be considered, for example on the exchange rate and the housing market as these will also have influenced household spending.

## 3. The effect of wealth

Theories such as the Keynesian absolute income hypothesis stress the importance of current income as a determinant of consumption. However, household finances are influenced by wealth as well as income.

- Income is a **flow** concept: it represents earnings over a given period of time, for example an annual salary for a worker or a monthly rent for a landlord.

- Wealth is a **stock** concept: it represents a value of financial worth at a period of time, for example the value of a property or a share in a company.

Wealth can be affected by increases in asset values, most typically resulting from a boom in the housing market or stock market.

2003 saw massive house price inflation as we noted in Chapter 1. Figure 1.15 showed 22.4% on the Halifax index and 19.4% on the Nationwide index. This large increase represented a significant boost to perceived household wealth. The UK housing market was also experiencing a buy-to-let boom, with many people choosing to divert savings from more traditional financial assets (savings accounts and pension funds) and into second homes, which would then provide an income stream (rent) in addition to an increase in value.

2003 saw a more difficult year for the stock market. The FTSE index fell by over 10% as oil prices increased and concerns grew surrounding conflict in the Middle East and tension in North Korea. However, even as the UK housing market cooled, the FTSE bounced back and recorded double-digit gains until the recession of 2008-2009.

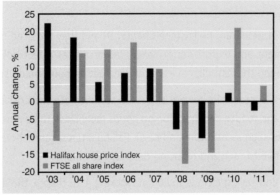

*Figure 2.5:Halifax house price index and FTSE all share index*

Source: HM Treasury

The housing market has a particularly powerful effect on the economy in the UK. Unlike other countries in Europe, the UK has a high proportion of owner occupied homes, with at least 50% of homes owner occupied in all regions, and some regions with over 70% owner occupation (see Figure 2.6). This makes consumption more responsive to changes in interest rates (via the impact on mortgage repayments) and to changes in house prices (via wealth effects – positive when house prices rise, but negative when house prices fall).

The debate over the influence of house prices on the wider economy is controversial. If house prices fall, this reduces the wealth of home owners, but it will also reduce the cost of borrowing for first time buyers which in theory leaves more disposable income for other areas of spending. In addition, lower house prices

*Figure 2.6: Housing tenure by region, UK 2008-2009, %*

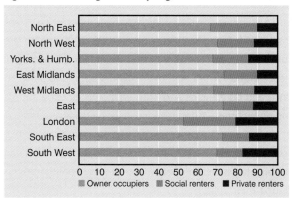

Source: ONS

represent a lower cost to landlords in the buy-to-let sector, which according to market theory should reduce the cost of renting and again increase consumption on non-housing goods.

A final consideration is that of mortgage equity withdrawal. A homeowner experiencing positive equity (where the market price of their home is greater than the value of mortgage debt outstanding) can, in theory, remortgage their house to free up funds for spending. This can be used for consumption or the purchase of another property for own use or to lease for rental income.

During the NICE decade, the concept of the housing market as a source of extra income and a means of saving for retirement became widespread. This was exacerbated by various factors:

● High house price inflation, outstripping returns from more traditional savings.

● Price inelastic supply of housing in urban areas.

● Demographic changes, increasing the proportion of one-person households.

● A severe decline in confidence in pension schemes after high-profile scandals such as Mirror Group (1991) and Equitable Life (2004).

● A significant increase in global money supply which led to easy credit terms, banks' acceptance of rising loan-to-value ratios, and low interest rates which discouraged saving and reduced borrowing rates.

● Income elastic demand for housing as it is seen as a superior alternative to the 'inferior' good of renting a home.

### 4. Other factors

The impact of globalisation on the UK economy was an important factor during the NICE decade and beyond. Related issues including migration, greater interconnectedness of international trade and the continued rise of the multinational corporation all played their part in shaping opportunities and threats for UK households, firms and the government.

Key impacts of globalisation have been:

● Cheaper money in world credit markets due to higher saving ratios in emerging economies such as China.

● Falling prices of consumer durables due to lower labour and land costs for growing businesses in Newly Industrialising Countries (NICs), and lower costs for UK-based firms engaging in *off-shoring* (moving business functions to cheaper countries) and *outsourcing* (contracting business functions to be supplied by a cheaper, foreign supplier).

● Greater migration, both into (immigration) and out of (emigration) the UK; this has helped to fill skills gaps in the UK labour market and to offer opportunities for some UK workers to move abroad.

Government policy can also influence consumption levels in the economy. Monetary policy clearly influences the key decision whether to spend or save for households and firms, but fiscal policy also affects the incentives to work, earn, save and invest through marginal rates of income tax, tax relief on pension saving, and corporation tax and tax breaks for firms.

### Question

2. Using the data given above, which model – or combination of models – provides the most accurate theory of what factors influence consumer spending in the economy?

## ● Analysis: **Why did consumer spending collapse in 2008-2009?**

As noted in Chapter 1 consumer spending is the single largest component of GDP, and it is therefore no surprise that the fall in GDP experienced during the recession of 2008-2009 can be largely explained by a drop in consumption. The relationship between consumption, GDP and investment can be analysed by two effects: the multiplier and the accelerator. When economic growth begins to slow, this influences both consumer and business confidence and households and firms change their expectations of future income levels. Investment – capital spending by firms – often responds more quickly and more drastically. Firms do not need to invest; supermarket chains expecting tougher trading conditions can call a halt to expansion, and manufacturers and construction firms will reduce output in anticipation of lower demand. This is called the **accelerator effect**, and is often a key indicator that an economy is heading into recession even before consumers and governments change their behaviour.

Households tend to react more slowly to changes in economic circumstance. The various economic theories of consumption explained in the section at the beginning of this chapter show that the correlation between income, and income expectations, and consumer spending is not perfect. However, a drop in investment (or a fall in other injections into the circular flow, such as government spending or net exports) reduces GDP, in turn affecting household's abilities to afford to maintain existing standards of living. The recession of 2008-2009 was in many ways a casebook in how recession leads to falling consumer spending, with the addition of some other factors which compounded the problems already facing households.

### ● Falling disposable incomes

However imperfect, the link between spending and earnings is nonetheless important. Recession led to rising unemployment, directly reducing average earnings, and even workers who remained in employment often faced wage freezes and lower bonuses and commission than had been available during the previous boom. In addition, CPI inflation remained stubbornly high despite negative growth, eroding the real value of incomes as prices increased faster than average earnings.

### ● Negative wealth effects

The housing market experienced dramatic 'corrections' as the bubble burst. Despite unprecedented reductions in the base rate of interest, which reduced the burden of debt on owner-occupiers with variable mortgage repayments, households experienced a reduction in wealth as the market value of their homes fell. This was exacerbated by the inflow of funds into the buy-to-let market during 'the NICE decade', and was matched by losses in stock market values which further reduced the wealth and confidence of households.

### ● Tougher credit conditions

Despite reductions in the base rate of interest by the Bank of England, the actual costs of financing credit cards and mortgages rose. Banks became less willing to lend as they attempted to address the bad debts on their books, and when lending was available the risk premium was often increased to reflect the difficult trading conditions in the financial sector. This disconnection between the base rate and market rates of interest was known as '**decoupling**', and raises serious questions about the effectiveness of monetary policy in managing demand during a credit crisis.

### ● Higher saving ratio

Despite falling incomes, downturn and recession is often accompanied by an increase in the saving ratio as households increase precautionary balances in case of job losses, and also to try to bring down debt levels if they predict negative equity on their home. Figure 1.14 from the previous chapter (repeated here as Figure 2.7) shows this effect clearly. The problem is further compounded as consumers reduce their discretionary spending (purchasing of non-essential goods and services), leading to lower demand and job losses for suppliers of these 'luxury' goods.

*Figure 2.7: UK saving ratio*

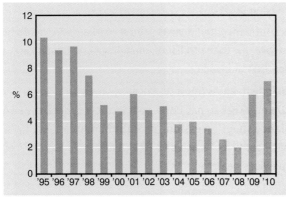

Source: HM Treasury

## ● Commodity price rises

Prices of oil and food products increased in 2008, reducing the ability of households to buy other goods and services. Low income households in particular are affected significantly by higher food and energy prices.

### Question

3. What is meant by the terms 'food poverty' and 'fuel poverty' in an economy such as the UK? Why are these problems of greater significance during recession?

## ● ● Application and Analysis: Explaining changes in the pattern of saving in the UK

Perhaps counter-intuitively, between 1995 and 2008 (except for a few minor increases) UK households saved a falling proportion of incomes. However, once the economy entered recession, the ratio increased by 250%, from 2% to 7% by 2010. Clearly, the concept of a stable **average propensity** or **marginal propensity to save** is highly dubious.

The different reasons for saving are important to explore at this stage.

Households save to defer present consumption and fund future consumption (e.g. saving for a future holiday or to buy high-price consumer durables, or when waiting for prices to fall), to prepare for retirement (e.g. saving in a pension fund), and as a means of avoiding future drops in consumption if income expectations are uncertain (precautionary saving). It is this latter factor which best explains the UK saving ratio over the last 15 years.

In times of strong economic growth, and when households expect such growth to continue, households may save a lower proportion of income as the need to build up precautionary balances declines. In essence, households believe they are less likely to be jobless, and thus feel free to spend a higher proportion of what they earn.

Other factors also reduced the saving ratio up to 2007:

● Historically low interest rates encouraged borrowing and discouraged saving in the UK.

● Relatively high interest rates pushed up the value of sterling and pushed down the prices of imported goods, helping to fuel a consumer boom.

● Rising house prices increased positive equity in property, reducing the need for households to save income to build up wealth levels.

During the most recent recessions of 2008-2009 and 2012, the rise in the saving ratio can perhaps be best explained by the precautionary saving model.

- Low consumer and business confidence and a weak labour market have made households wary of spending and more inclined to save due to the threat of unemployment. Despite very low rates of return, saving has increased as a proportion of income.

- Households with high levels of indebtedness (most significantly where large loans were taken out to buy housing at peak prices in 2007) may seek to pay down debt levels to reduce their exposure to negative equity. This is known as a '**balance sheet recession**', or '**debt hangover**': even where positive income growth has resumed, economic agents feel a negative wealth effect through property and other asset prices remaining below their previous peak.

## ● Application: **Saving – an international dimension**

*Figure 2.8: International comparison of household saving ratios (% average 2001-2011)*

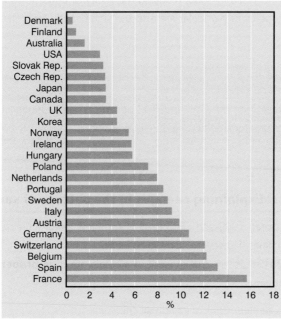

Source: OECD

As already shown, the household saving ratio for an economy can fluctuate considerably over time. In addition, different countries can have very different average saving ratios.

It should be noted that for some of these economies (Australia and Denmark; also experienced in Greece), the saving ratio was negative over some of the period over which the average was calculated.

Traditionally, saving was seen as beneficial for both individuals and firms. Saving leads to higher deposits in the banking sector, and these funds can then be lent out to borrowers for mortgages or business investment. However, as international global money flows have increased, and firms as well as economies have become more globalised, this reliance on domestic bank deposits to fund domestic investment has weakened.

## ● Knowledge: **The paradox of thrift – should more saving be encouraged?**

John Maynard Keynes popularised the concept of the **paradox of thrift**; that every decision to save, rather than spend, reduces demand in the economy and therefore causes demand-deficient unemployment. This is encapsulated by the quote, 'Whenever you save five shillings, you put a man out of work for a day.'

However, the Governor of the Bank of England, Mervyn King, said in 2009 that, 'the United Kingdom faces... fundamental long-run challenge(s)... to rebalance the economy, with more resources allocated to business investment and net exports and fewer to consumption. That is consistent with the need – now widely accepted – to eliminate the large structural fiscal deficit and to raise the national saving rate.'[1]

The paradox of thrift appears to suggest that higher saving will reduce demand and reduce economic growth further. However, this assumes that higher savings create only lower demand, and are not used to create extra borrowing, which in turn stimulates purchases of consumer durables and business investment. The efficiency of the financial industry in creating credit is therefore an important factor in determining whether the higher saving ratio in recent years has been harmful or not. In the same speech quoted above,

---

1. http://www.bankofengland.co.uk/publications/Documents/speeches/2009/speech406.pdf

Mervyn King proposed the second challenge facing the UK was to reform the structure and regulation of the banking sector. He has since made calls for banks to lend more money to smaller businesses, providing essential credit for firms to expand and create jobs and profit.

## Question

4. "Higher saving is hindering, not helping the UK economy at present." To what extent do you agree with this statement?

## ● Analysis: **The Pensions Crisis: an even bigger problem?**

*Figure 2.9: UK life expectancy at birth (2012-2020 projections)*

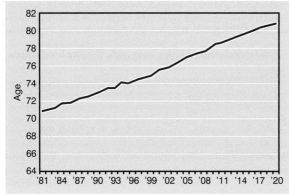

Source: ONS

*Figure 2.10: UK births (p.a.)*

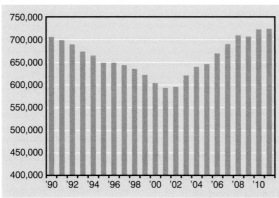

Source: ONS

*Figure 2.11: Births by age of mother (as % of births p.a.)*

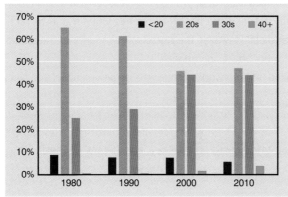

Source: ONS

As important a role as savings play in the success of the macroeconomy, one area of concern in many highly developed economies is that of pension provision. A pension is a saving device to allow households to put money aside during their working years to fund retirement. Traditionally, workers would be employed by only a small number of firms (and often only one) over their working life, and powerful trade unions negotiated generous pensions based on final salary. The state pension – payments to old age pensioners, regardless of household income and wealth – was also an important element of the welfare state since 1945.

Various factors have created a potential pension crisis for the UK:

● Increased life expectancy (Figure 2.9).

● For some years, the UK experienced a falling birth rate (Figure 2.10).

● Increased numbers of people extending their education past the compulsory school-leaving age, meaning later entry into the labour market.

● These two factors have also contributed to a shift towards families having children at a later age, leading to 'generational stretch' (Figure 2.11 shows the proportion of births to mothers over the age of 40 has risen four-fold since 1980).

● Greater labour market mobility and a breakdown of the 'job for life' culture has increased the likely number of employers in a worker's lifetime – reducing the ability of workers to build up a substantial pension saving.

- Loss of confidence in traditional pension schemes.

- Higher yields from other forms of 'saving', such as the buy-to-let market during the housing boom in the second half of the NICE decade.

- Lower interest rates for savers, especially since the drastic cuts in the base rate in 2009.

European countries where a 'pensions timebomb' are predicted to take place during the 21st century include the UK, Italy and Spain. A combination of high youth unemployment, high housing costs and a shift in culture away from 'traditional' family values may leave the economy short of workers (and therefore tax-payers) at a time when the cost of supporting an ageing population rise dramatically, given improvements in healthcare and rising life expectancies.

Figure 2.10 shows that, for the UK, the number of births has actually been rising since 2001. Some of this is due to greater immigration and higher birth rates in migrant families.

Policies which could be used to tackle the pensions timebomb problem include:

- Higher state pension retirement age (the age at which a state pension can be collected).

- Means-tested state pension (higher income households – typically those with significant private pensions – will no longer receive state pensions).

- Less generous state pension payments in real terms.

- Greater incentives to save for a pension, e.g. higher tax relief on employee and employer contributions.

- Extensive public information campaigns to alert young workers to the importance of preparing for retirement.

- Greater labour market flexibility to allow older workers to remain working, perhaps in part-time or flexible capacities.

- Compulsory employer pension contributions.

- A minimum retirement age for private as well as state pension funds.

- A 'laissez-faire' approach, where older workers who have not saved sufficiently will have no choice but to continue working or depend on other benefits, e.g. disability or sickness payments.

- Compulsory individual pension tax (this has been introduced in Australia).

The pension issue is a very good example of how long-term problems which require long-term solutions are often ignored by governments of the day. **Public choice theory** suggests that governments do not, in reality, aim to maximise social welfare, but rather seek re-election by 'buying' votes with policies which appeal to their core electorate. The likely popularity of the policies listed above offers an insight into the likelihood of core reforms taking place before more drastic decisions have to be made.

One important point to consider is whether these projected increases in life expectancy will actually occur. Highly developed societies may actually see health outcomes worsen due to factors such as stress, sedentary lifestyles, and high-fat diets. However, the worse case scenario for the public finances would be an increase in healthcare costs for the obese and unhealthy, but a continued rise in life expectancy: people could stay sicker for longer while unable to work, with drastic negative impacts on NHS and care costs.

### Question Extension

5. The Australian government introduced a compulsory 'pension tax' in the 1990s.

    Evaluate the case for and against such a policy in the UK.

# Chapter 3

# Business and Industry

● ● Knowledge **and** Application: **The structure of the UK economy**

The term **economic growth** refers to increases in the productive capacity of an economy: how increases in the quantity and quality of factors of production can lead to higher output levels and a rising standard of living.

Over the past 300 years, the structure of the UK economy has undergone radical change. Modern economies such as the UK have typically experienced a series of 'revolutions' during which the dominant industries for employment and output have changed dramatically.

### 1. Industrial revolution

As new technologies in the *primary sector* (agricultural and energy extraction industries) developed, this liberated some land, labour and capital for use in the emerging *secondary sector* (manufacturing). Large numbers of households moved from the countryside to towns and cities to work in factories and mills. Thus **industrialisation** occurred alongside **urbanisation** and the manufacturing sector grew in importance throughout the 19th and 20th centuries. In terms of the agricultural sector, by 2012 60% of the UK's food needs were produced domestically by less than 2% of the workforce.

### 2. Post-industrial revolution

By the 1970s and 1980s, it was clear that the UK manufacturing sector was facing increasing competition from the resurgent economies of Germany and Japan, other trading partners within the expanding European Economic Community (the precursor to today's European Union) and from newly-industrialising countries such as Taiwan. The process of **deindustrialisation** saw British manufacturing face serious decline, as either UK-based firms moved production overseas, were driven out of business, or were absorbed into multinational conglomerates through merger or takeover.

Between 1997 and 2007, manufacturing output in the UK fell from 28% to 12% of GDP and manufacturing employment fell from one in four workers to one in ten. These changes were almost perfectly matched by an equivalent growth in service sector output and employment. However, as of 2009 the manufacturing sector employed 2.6 million British workers and the UK remained the world's sixth largest exporter by value of output, and a major exporter of technology-intensive manufactures. By 2000 the main threat to the UK's competitiveness in global manufacturing markets was the rapidly developing economies of China and India.

*Figure 3.1: Growth in industrial production, selected economies*

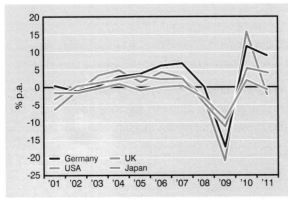

Source: HM Treasury

Figure 3.1 shows how UK industrial production growth compares with other regions and countries in recent years.

Clearly, all four of the economies shown in Figure 3.1 saw manufacturing output fall during the recession of 2008-09. The UK saw the lowest fall in output of those economies shown, but throughout the pre-recession period of 2001-07 the UK had the lowest average rate of growth (a contraction of 0.4%, compared with growth in the USA of 1.2%, 1.3% in Japan and 2.8% in Germany).

*Figure 3.2: Growth in industrial production, UK, compared with the G7 average*

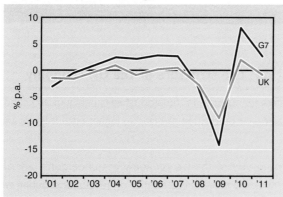

Source: HM Treasury

Figure 3.2 compares UK industrial growth with the G7 average. (The G7 group of countries comprises Canada, France, Germany, Italy, Japan, the USA and the UK.) Figure 3.2 shows that except for 2001 and 2009, the G7 average growth rate outstripped growth in the UK economy.

## ● Analysis: **Why has the UK experienced deindustrialisation?**

Reasons for the decline in the importance of UK manufacturing within the UK and in global markets include:

● Loss of competitive advantage against lower-cost producers, including **newly-industrialising countries (NICs)** such as China, Taiwan, South Korea and Singapore.

● Loss of competitive advantage against other advanced economies. As Figure 3.3 shows, the UK's labour costs grew faster than the G7 average throughout the period, even in 2010 when the G7 level fell.

*Figure 3.3: UK and G7 unit labour costs in manufacturing*

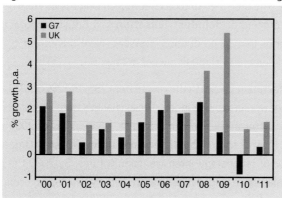

Source: HM Treasury

● Increasingly globalised markets for traded goods which reduced transport costs to facilitate greater world trade.

● Relatively high land costs in the UK (linked to higher population density in urban areas).

● Relatively high labour costs in the UK (strong trade union power until the 1980s, and a higher standard of living and therefore higher cost of living).

● Weak investment in infrastructure, reducing the efficiency of national and international trading links.

## ● Evaluation: **Is manufacturing still important in the UK?**

The period of strong growth in the UK between the mid-1990s and 2007 was characterised by high levels of consumer demand, increased government expenditure, a falling saving ratio and a widening trade imbalance, as imports into the UK outstripped exports from the UK at a growing rate.

In May 2011, the Governor of the Bank of England, Mervyn King, was quoted as saying, *"The rebalancing of the UK economy which implies slow growth in consumer spending and in public spending will take not just one year but several years, and the switch to business investment and net exports will also take several years."*[1]

---

1. http://www.bbc.co.uk/blogs/thereporters/stephanieflanders/2011/05/inflation_up_growth_down_uncer.html

In common with many mature economies, the UK has experienced an expanding tertiary (service) sector as the secondary (manufacturing) sector has shrunk. This section will explore the key question: is the decline of manufacturing important?

The relevant factors to consider in answering this question include the following:

● Manufactured goods are easier to export than (most) services. The UK enjoys a strong position as a major provider of financial services such as banking and insurance and is also a major tourism destination (ranked sixth in the world) but other services are produced for predominantly domestic consumption, such as transport, healthcare and retail.

● Chapter 5, which examines the current account of the balance of payments, offers more detail regarding the balance of internationally traded goods and services. Figure 5.1 shows that trade in services has been in surplus (exports from the UK have exceeded imports into the UK) over every one of the past 20 years, whereas the trade in goods has been in deficit. It is important to note that the services surplus has been smaller than the goods deficit – a major contributor to the current account deficit in recent years.

● A shrinking manufacturing sector can also explain a relative decline in UK productivity. Technological innovation can increase productivity, usually by allowing labour (which can be expensive in a country such as the UK, where the cost of living is high) for cheaper capital (which, in the present century, can increasingly be produced in low-wage, low-rent NICs). Such substitution, however, is more difficult in the service sector industries where the UK enjoys a competitive advantage, such as tourism or financial services. Figure 3.4 shows how, despite the impact of recession on the data for 2009, manufacturing productivity growth has outstripped service sector productivity growth in recent years.

*Figure 3.4: Productivity in UK manufacturing and service sectors (index, 2006 = 100)*

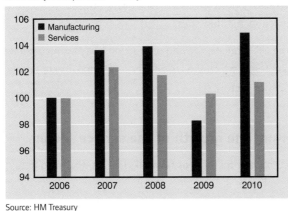

Source: HM Treasury

● A strong manufacturing sector can also stimulate a culture of innovation and investment. This is linked to the point above: the possibility of high returns from capital spending acts as an incentive for firms to spend on research and development (R&D) which can be a key driver of long-run, supply-side growth for the macroeconomy.

● Finally, manufacturing still accounts for 60% of the value of UK exports. The pattern of exports of goods from the UK (see Figure 3.5) gives a clear indication of the competitiveness and value of the manufacturing sectors of the UK economy.

*Figure 3.5: UK exports of manufactured goods in 2009, £m*

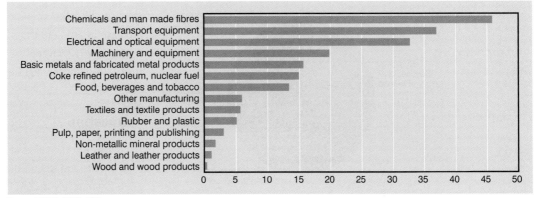

Source: MQ10, 2010, ONS

The UK clearly still enjoys a strong position as an exporter of manufactured goods such as chemicals and fibres and transport and electrical equipment. In addition, manufacturing activity creates jobs in related service sector industries such as transport, distribution and finance. The UK does still enjoy world dominance in some sectors, such as the production of Formula 1 cars and other high-technology industries.

However, there are other arguments regarding the importance, and even desirability, of sustaining UK manufacturing to consider.

*Figure 3.6: UK net profitability, secondary and tertiary sector*

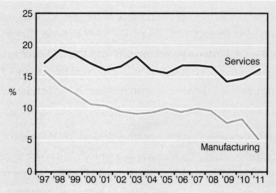

Source: ONS

- Figure 3.6 compares the net profitability of manufacturing and service sector forms in the UK since 1997. Profitability – the ability of firms to turn capital employed into profit – is higher in the service sector, and the differential has widened in recent years.

- Export-led growth may not improve the current account position significantly if UK production depends on imported raw materials or even, in some cases, off-shored and outsourced production and services.

- Policies to boost UK production of manufactures may distort the market and lead to resources being wasted on relatively expensive and relatively low quality goods.

- A trade deficit in goods need not be a problem providing earnings from imports, investment income and transfers are sufficient to create an overall balance on the current account. Thus support which might be given to the manufacturing sector might be more efficiently utilised in bolstering already strong competitive advantages in service sector industries.

- Arguably, structural shifts in the UK economy moving production away from manufacturing and towards services represent strong market forces which the UK and its policy-makers are powerless to totally resist (see the next section on the service sector).

● ● **Knowledge and Application: The growth of the service sector**

Service sector output in 2012 accounted for 77% of UK GDP. Of this, the main industries were business services and finance as is shown in Figure 3.7.

Between 2009 and 2012, the two largest contributors to the UK service sector also grew the fastest: business services and finance (3.5%) and government (3.6%). In terms of the latter, this was boosted considerably by a 12.7% increase in arts, entertainment & recreation output in 2012. Overall, service sector output rose 1.1% between 2011 and 2012.

*Figure 3.7: Service sector industries*

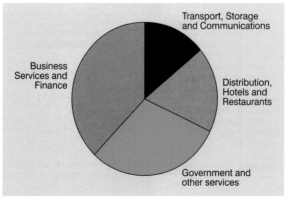

Source: ONS

**Question**

1. Why did the value of arts, entertainment and recreation increase so dramatically in 2012?

## ● ● Knowledge and Application: Investment in the UK

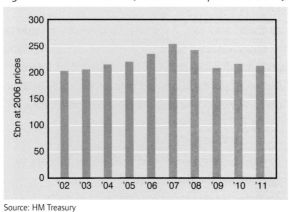

*Figure 3.8: UK investment (Gross Fixed Capital Formation)*

Source: HM Treasury

Investment plays a crucial role in any economy. As a significant component of aggregate demand, investment spending contributes to GDP and therefore the overall health of the macroeconomy through creating output and jobs. Investment is also a key driver of long-run trend growth, increasing productivity and productive potential. The key measure of investment is Fixed Capital Investment: spending on producer goods (or capital goods) such as machinery, ICT and plant which is then used to produce consumer goods or other producer goods.

## ● Analysis: Why is investment volatile?

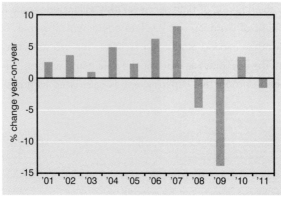

*Figure 3.9: UK investment*

Source: HM Treasury

Investment levels in the economy are seen by economists as an important indicator of the future expectations of firms. If business confidence is strong, firms are prepared to commit spending to increasing their production and supply potential. But when confidence is weak they will stop new investment projects (and even in extreme cases, mothball current projects) as they anticipate flat or falling demand in the future. Figure 3.9 shows the annual percentage change in investment levels over the same period as that shown in Figure 3.8. Invest-ment levels fall by almost 5% in 2008, followed by a drop of over 10% in 2009. Investment in 2009 had fallen by 18% in real terms from its peak in 2007, reducing the contribution made to GDP by investment from 17.3% to 15%.

Investment spending tends to be more volatile than other components of GDP, such as consumption and government spending, for various reasons:

### ● The accelerator effect

Investment spending often reacts more quickly and more dramatically than spending by households and the public sector. This was discussed in more detail in Chapter 2, where causes of the fall in consumer spending in 2008-09 is discussed. In brief, firms can reduce investment more easily than households can do with consumer spending. A high proportion of household consumption, particularly for those on lower incomes, is called **autonomous consumption**. Mortgage payments or rent, and spending on food and energy are difficult to change in the short-run without significant adjustments to lifestyles, and therefore even when average incomes fall in the economy there may be a period where household spending does not keep up with this change.

Similarly, governments are committed to both **current spending** (public sector wages and other running costs) and **capital spending** (public sector investment in infrastructure and nationalised sectors). Capital projects can, of course, be mothballed, but for reasons of demand-management this may be a difficult policy to implement particularly when economic growth is falling or even negative.

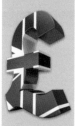

### • Rates of return

Investment has to be paid for, and firms will generally do this by either borrowing money from a bank, issuing corporate bonds or using previous profits (retained profit).

The rate of interest charged by banks can vary according to changes in monetary policy and the competitiveness and health of the financial sector. Since the credit crisis of 2007, many small and medium sized firms in the UK have complained that credit is difficult to find, and interest rates are too high. Similarly, the rate of return offered on corporate bonds will be determined by both prevailing returns, or rates of interest in the credit markets, as well as the appetite bond purchasers have for risk.

### • Retained profits

An alternative to borrowing is to fund business expansion from the profits accrued in previous years. Retained profit is likely to be higher during the boom stage of the economic cycle, which explains why investment can rise so dramatically during a period of rapid economic expansion. The data in Figure 3.9 for 2006 and 2007 shows annual investment growth of over 5% in real terms. In addition to strong growth, this was also a period when interest rates in the UK were relatively low.

### • Technology

It is important to distinguish between **gross profit** and **net profit**. Gross profit is simply total spending on capital goods by firms over a given period of time. However, this will include some of what economists call **depreciation**: the replacement of worn-out or obsolete equipment. If a high proportion of gross investment goes to replace rather than expand production facilities, this will not increase the productive capacity of the firm (and, indeed, the economy) as much as the data might suggest. Net investment is the term used for the overall change in productive capacity, and is calculated as gross investment minus depreciation.

## Question

2. In periods of rapid technological change, such as the industrial revolution, explain why investment might be high. And why might net investment be considerably lower?

*Investment spending on items such as machinery and plant is very volatile and depends on business confidence.*

## Knowledge and Application: Foreign Direct Investment

*Figure 3.10: Net inward FDI to the UK*

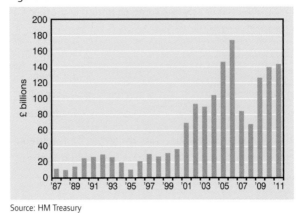

Source: HM Treasury

Foreign Direct Investment (FDI) refers to cross-border investment activities by **multinational companies** (**MNC**s). FDI can be outward (where UK firms invest in plant overseas) or inward (where foreign firms invest in the UK). Globally, FDI was $1.9 trillion in 2007. This figure fell during the crises of 2008 and 2009, but is expected to be approximately $1.6 trillion in 2012. Despite expansion by UK firms abroad, the UK is a net recipient of FDI funds as shown in Figure 3.10.

## Analysis: Why is FDI important?

The advantages of FDI for the UK are:

- Inwards FDI is an injection into the circular flow of income and thus creates output and jobs, both directly and indirectly through the supply chain.

- This economic activity will create tax revenues for the UK government from VAT and income taxes.

- The inflow of funds contributes to the UK's surplus on the financial account of the balance of payments.

- Multinationals bring new knowledge and technology to the UK, creating higher productivity gains which can spill over into domestic firms.

The disadvantages of FDI for the UK are:

- Profits made in the UK by a foreign firm may be repatriated to the head office, which is likely to be overseas. MNCs with interests in the UK may therefore pay no or very little corporation tax to the Treasury. Repatriated profits, and earnings by foreign executives living in the UK, will be a debit on the financial account of the balance of payments.

- Foreign firms compete with domestic firms, which may lead to job losses (particularly if the MNC enjoys higher productivity and the economies of scale associated with large organisations).

- MNCs aim to maximise profits, and therefore will choose to operate in economies where the tax regime is favourable to the firm and its employees. It can be argued, therefore, that attempts to maintain FDI can constrain domestic fiscal policy, such as a specific levy on banking.

- MNCs are mobile, or 'footloose', and may therefore leave whenever trading conditions determine they might be more profitably located elsewhere. This can cause structural unemployment, which is usually geographically concentrated.

## Analysis: Why is the UK an attractive destination for FDI?

The non-inflationary growth of the NICE decade and the acceptance of the importance of globalisation by the New Labour government made the UK one of the main recipients of FDI in recent years (25% of inward FDI in the EU; the UK was second to only the USA as the largest recipient of global FDI in 1998).

Other factors making the UK attractive are:

- A highly-skilled labour force, particularly in financial services and some high technology manufacturing sectors.

● Membership of the European Union, meaning any output exported from the UK to other EU countries is classed as a British export and therefore is not subject to the Common External Tariff (import tax).

● The UK labour market is more flexible and lightly regulated than in many other European economies, making it easier and cheaper for MNCs to recruit workers here.

The recession in 2008 reduced FDI considerably as Figure 3.10 makes clear, before rebounding in 2010 and 2011, possibly because these challenging macroeconomic conditions were experienced throughout the EU and the UK remained an attractive place to invest. Relative to the performance of 'the PIIGS' (Portugal, Ireland, Italy, Greece and Spain), the UK has arguably gained a competitive advantage.

Some economists have argued that although Britain's position inside the EU is a strength in attracting FDI, its reluctance to adopt the single European currency (the euro) is a weakness. In the light of the uncertain future of the eurozone (see Chapter 12) this argument needs less consideration.

Other weaknesses perceived for the UK are:

● A rising tax burden, which makes the UK a less attractive place to work and do business.

● An increase in business bureaucracy ('red-tape').

*Figure 3.11: Where does UK inward FDI come from? (2010)*

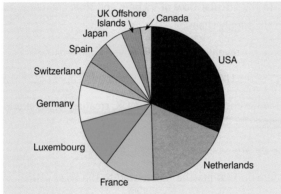

Source: ONS

*Figure 3.12: Where does UK outward FDI take place? (2010)*

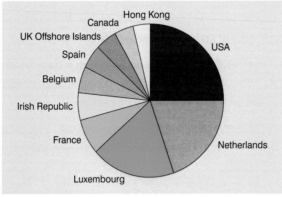

Source: ONS

Again, this needs to be viewed in the context of other Western European economies which tend to have similar, if not more restrictive, business environments.

In recent years there has been growing interest in the growth of sovereign wealth funds. This is usually oil revenue which creates wealth for economies such as Saudi Arabia or Norway, which can then be used to invest in global business opportunities. Interestingly, Figure 3.11 shows that the major contributors to UK inward FDI are none of the rapidly growing BRIC countries or major oil-producing nations.

Figure 3.12 shows the pattern of UK outwards FDI.

For both inward and outward flows, the EU, North America and Japan account for almost all of the top ten countries shown.

## Question

3. Does it matter that the BRIC nations and the oil-producing countries are not major sources of inward FDI to the UK?

## ●● Knowledge **and** Application: **The UK stock market**

The performance of the UK stock market in recent years was shown in Figure 1.9 in Chapter 1. The stock market offers an insight into the performance of the largest firms in the economy, most of which have

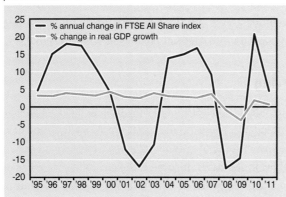

Figure 3.13: Real GDP growth and stock market performance for the UK

Source: HM Treasury

publicly-owned shares. These shares (which are a *share* of ownership, and entitle holders to a *share* of the profits made) are traded on the stock market. Aggregate measures such as the FTSE indices show how the values of those firms are changing, based mainly on their fundamental ability to generate future profits. Therefore we might expect stock market performance to correlate closely with overall macroeconomic performance, measured best as real GDP growth. Figure 3.13 shows the movement in real GDP growth in the UK with the annual change in stock market prices.

The '**bull markets**' of 1996-2000 and 2004-2007 can be viewed with hindsight as examples of stock market bubbles, and fit into the wider picture presented in Chapter 1 of a period of very high consumption growth in the UK, fuelled by wealth effects from the housing market and stock markets. When UK (and global) growth appeared to falter after the 2000 dot-com crash, the UK stock market fell dramatically (this is known as a '**bear market**'), before recovering strongly in the years before the credit crisis and recession at the end of the 2000s.

Interestingly, the percentage loss experienced on the FTSE index in 2002 was just as severe as that seen in 2008, when the UK economy was in recession. At the end of 2003 the FTSE All Share Index stood at less than 2000, and even with double-dip recession in 2012 the stock market has continued to recover and maintain month-end levels higher than that seen in December 2011 (index of 2815).

Stock market volatility tends to be far greater than growth volatility. This trend has persisted throughout history, and was named 'animal spirits' by John Maynard Keynes: a form of herd behaviour where speculators over-react to the potential gains, and losses, in rapidly changing asset markets. This can be contrasted with the 'wisdom of crowds' theory, where aggregate opinions and behaviours are seen as more perceptive and rational than individual decisions.

## Question

4. Figure 3.13 shows the volatile character of stock market prices compared with the growth in the real economy. To explain this greater volatility the stockmarket has been described as "a market not in the present but in the future". How does that description help to account for the contrasting data in Figure 3.13?

# Chapter 4

# Living Standards, Poverty and Inequality

This chapter examines the changes in living standards over the past decade, looking at various measures of living standards. Measures of inequality and poverty are then examined, along with trends in inequality and poverty over the past decade. Following this there is a discussion on recent government policy to tackle poverty and inequality, concluding with a look at regional differences within the UK.

## ● Knowledge: **Standard of living**

There is considerable debate amongst economists about how best to measure standard of living. Many factors influence people's living standards. These include social, environmental, and political factors as well as economic ones. However, the vast majority of economists agree that a person or household's income is a very important determinant of living standards. **Income** is the sum of all the earnings received through employing factors of production in a given period of time. Crucially, income is a **flow** of earnings. Income could be in the form of wages, salaries, profits, interest payments, rents and other forms of earnings received.

## ● Application: **The rise and then 'squeeze' on living standards in the last decade**

*Figure 4.1: Growth in UK real household disposable income at 2009 prices*

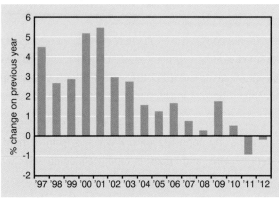

Source ONS    *Estimate for 2012 based on ONS data

'Real' household income growth is the growth in household income received accounting for the effects of inflation. So the data above shows the rate at which the average household's purchasing power has changed over the last 15 years. During the late 1990s at the time of the Labour government's first term in office, household incomes grew rapidly, but there was a marked slowdown in real income growth from 2002 onwards. Perhaps the most surprising part of the data above is that average real household incomes continued to grow during the recession of 2008-09, when GDP and employment fell considerably. Look back at Figure 1.1 to show the marked fall in GDP at this time. During these two years, household incomes were supported by a combination of growth in income from tax credits and state benefits, along with stable employment income and low inflation (according to the RPI index inflation was actually negative in 2009). However, the effects of the recession were delayed, not evaded. As the recovery faltered in 2010 and unemployment rose above 8%, workers had little bargaining power and average wage growth remains anaemic. Many workers accepted pay cuts or pay freezes. In addition, high cost-push inflationary pressures from rising petrol, food, clothing and energy prices eroded real household incomes. In September 2011 CPI inflation reached 5.2%, but then it fell sharply towards the 2.0% target by mid 2012, raising hopes that real income growth might be restored in the near future. However, there are several reasons to be pessimistic about this prospect. As the UK economy entered a second recession (look back at Figure 1.20) and continues to suffer from the ill-effects of the Eurozone crisis coupled with a 'debt drag', unemployment is set to remain high, meaning workers are in a weak bargaining position. Furthermore, the coalition's deficit reduction plans will implement net tax rises and cuts to benefits, which will further 'squeeze' real household incomes. Recent research by the Institute for Fiscal Studies (IFS) suggests that median real household income may be lower in the 2015-16 financial years than in 2002-3.

If this does occur, it would represent the worst period of change for median household income since at least the early 1960s.

*Table 4.1: Real GDP per capita and Real Household income compared across parliaments*

| Government | Real GDP per Capita (% change) | Real household disposable income per head (% change) |
|---|---|---|
| **Conservative 1979 to 1996-7** | 2.0 | 2.6 |
| **Labour 1996-7 to 2009-10** | 1.8 | 1.9 |
| *of which:* | | |
| Fast growth (1996-97 to 2001-02) | 3.3 | 3.4 |
| Weak growth (2001-02 to 2007-08) | 2.4 | 1.2 |
| Recent recession (2007-08 to 2009-10) | -3.6 | 0.7 |
| **Labour & Coalition: 2009-10 to 2010-11** | 1.4 | -2.8 |

Source: Cribb, Joyce & Phillip, *Living Standards, Inequality and Poverty in the UK 2012*, IFS

The data above confirms that although the 2008-09 recession caused GDP to fall sharply, real household incomes have been hit hardest in the years following the end of that recession in 2009.

Although there are various ways in which living standards can be measured, real GDP per capita is the measure most commonly used by economists. There are however, limitations to the use of this measure. These include:

● No account taken for the distribution of income and wealth – GDP per capita is a crude 'mean' measure, and so it might not give an accurate reflection of the income of an 'average' person in a country, especially if income is distributed unevenly. If a large share of national income is concentrated at the top end of the income distribution, then the mean GDP per capita figure will be higher than the true income of the 'average' person. Therefore, a measure of median income might be a better reflection of the income of an 'average' person.

● No account taken for externalities – growth often occurs with resulting negative externalities (e.g. pollution) but these are not accounted for in GDP figures. Thus, growth in GDP may overstate the resultant rise in living standards.

● Quality changes ignored – over time the quality of goods and services tend to increase but these are not accounted for in GDP figures. Therefore, rises in the quality of goods and services (e.g. safer cars, better quality TVs etc.) means that increases in living standards may be greater than a crude GDP per capita measure suggests.

● No account taken for the 'balance' of growth – growth based on consumption today may take available resources away from investment, which would bring faster growth tomorrow. The UK economy has become very dependant on consumption, as was discussed in Chapter 1. Since the financial crisis in 2008 policy makers have emphasised the importance of a 'rebalancing' of the economy away from consumption and importing, towards investment and exports.

● Exports are valued more highly than imports – In GDP statistics the value of exports is added to GDP while the value of imports is subtracted from GDP, as shown in the formula C + I + G + (X-M). So, according to GDP data imports subtract from living standards, which plainly isn't true in many cases. If UK citizens enjoy a foreign made car, or some fine French wine, in reality this will add to, rather than detract from, living standards.

● No account for the underground economy – illegal activities such as drug dealing along with any cash-in hand activities not declared to the tax authorities are not included in GDP statistics. In 2012 the size

of the UK underground economy was estimated to be around 11% of GDP. This figure compares favourably with other European economies, i.e. is lower, suggesting a high degree of tax compliance.

- No account taken for non-marketed items – if you carry out some DIY work on your home, or someone babysits for you free of charge, these services will not be counted in GDP statistics, but if you pay for these (or similar services), they will be counted.

- No account taken for the opportunity cost of growth – in order to create growth leisure time may be foregone. By working longer hours GDP may increase, but living standards might not.

- Errors in calculation are likely – GDP data is calculated using tax returns from millions of sources. There are bound to be errors and inaccuracies in the data.

### Exam Hint

When answering an exam question it may be relevant to explain some of the limitations of using GDP data to estimate living standards. It is always better to go for **depth** over **breadth**. Pick two or three limitations and explain them in detail, rather than explaining five limitations superficially.

## Alternative measures to income

The material 'standard' of living can be contrasted with '**quality of life**' which accounts for other, more intangible factors that affect human life, such as health, environmental quality, safety, social life, culture etc. Attempts to measure quality of life tend to give a better indicator of people's overall '**well-being**'.

The **Genuine Progress indicator** (**GPI**) is an extension of the **Index of Sustainable Economic Welfare** (**ISEW**). The GPI aims to account for the costs of the negative consequences of economic growth, as well as the positive impacts, and hence give a more balanced account of how the overall well being of a country's citizens have changed over time. The measure accounts for factors that the GDP measure ignores, such as:

- Cost of resource depletion
- Cost of crime
- Cost of ozone depletion
- Cost of family breakdown
- Cost of air, water, and noise pollution
- Loss of farmland
- Loss of wetlands

With such emphasis placed on environmental as well as social factors, it is unsurprising that the GPI is a popular measure amongst 'green' economists. The ISEW and GPI indicators show a diverging trend from the GDP measure since the 1970s for most rich economies, including the UK. The GPI failed to increase significantly since the 1970s, suggesting that rising incomes since the 1970s has come at the expense of high and unsustainable environmental and social costs, meaning that growth is now failing to add to the well-being of citizens in advanced economies. Of course, accurately measuring the cost of family breakdown and global warming is extremely difficult, and this is something that neo-classical economists point to when defending the GDP measure.

The United Nations first published the **Human Development Index** (**HDI**) in 1990. The HDI is composed of three indicators, and countries are given a score between 0 and 1. The indicators include:

- Real GDP per capita (using Purchasing Power Parity).

- Life expectancy at birth (to indicate the population's level of health and longevity).

- Educational attainment (measured using a weighted average of adult literacy rates and the gross enrolment ratio at primary, secondary and tertiary education level).

*Table 4.2: Selected HDI and GDP per capita data for 2011*

| Country | HDI Score | HDI ranking | GDP per capita (US$ PPP) | GDP per capita ranking | GDP per capita – HDI ranking |
|---------|-----------|-------------|---------------------------|-------------------------|-------------------------------|
| Norway | 0.943 | 1 | 47,557 | 7 | 6 |
| Australia | 0.929 | 2 | 34,431 | 18 | 16 |
| United States | 0.910 | 4 | 43,017 | 10 | 6 |
| UK | 0.863 | 28 | 33,296 | 21 | -7 |
| South Africa | 0.619 | 123 | 9,469 | 79 | -44 |
| Cuba | 0.776 | 51 | 5,416 | 103 | 52 |
| China | 0.687 | 101 | 7,476 | 94 | -7 |

Source: UN Human Development Report 2011

In Table 4.2 the final column showing the GDP per capita rank minus the HDI ranking for different countries is one way of examining whether higher incomes result in a higher quality of life for the citizens of that country. It is clearly not always the case that this occurs. South Africa has a GDP per capita ranking 44 places higher than its HDI ranking. This is due to the high rates of HIV/AIDS coupled with very high unemployment and poverty rates which reduce life expectancy considerably. In contrast Cuba has a very low ranking for GDP per capita owing to an inefficient command economy. However, Cuba's HDI ranking is 52 places higher due to an extensive literacy campaign and substantial public investment in healthcare. The UK's performance in the HDI rankings is hindered by a lower average number of years of schooling than other advanced economies, resulting in an HDI rank 7 places lower than her GDP per capita ranking.

## Evaluation of HDI as an indicator of living standards

| Advantages | Disadvantages |
|------------|---------------|
| The HDI goes beyond crude GDP measurements with all the associated limitations to incorporate statistics on education and healthcare, two key development goals. | The HDI is an aggregate measure which hides distribution. |
| The publishing of this indicator encourages countries to invest in education and healthcare. | Aggregate measures do little to tell us why HDI may have changed over time. |
| Unlike GDP an element of 'well being' is reflected in the statistics. | Wouldn't quality-adjusted life years (QALYs) be a better measure than simply the average number of years lived? |
| The HDI does not include too many indices and thus the problem of overlap is avoided e.g. infant mortality is not included but it's importance is reflected in the life expectancy indicator. | Shouldn't the quality of education be included, rather than just years in schooling? The UK has some of the best universities in the world, but this is not accounted for in the HDI measure. |
| The indices used are relatively easy to measure e.g. no value has to be placed on the cost of global warming. | Weightings given (equal for all 3 indicators) are fairly arbitrary. Some argue that income should be given more importance. |
| The UN now calculates the HDI to distinguish between regions, genders, and ethnic groups, thus avoiding 'broad brush' conclusions to be drawn based on aggregates. | The HDI may overstate development in countries with high inequality (e.g. Latin American countries) as aggregates mask the low quality of life endured by a large number. |

In 1999 the Labour Government committed itself to reporting annually on progress made towards sustainable development in the UK.

> "Talking about sustainable development is not enough. We have to know what it is, to see how our policies are working on the ground. We must hold to ourselves to account – as a government but also as a country… All this depends on devising new ways of assessing how we are doing."

**Tony Blair**

*A Better Quality of Life – A Strategy for Sustainable Development for the UK*, May 1999

This publication introduced 13 new headline indicators of quality of life: economic growth, social investment, employment, health, education and training, housing quality, climate change, air pollution, transport, water quality, wildlife, land use and finally waste.

In 2010 David Cameron asked the Office of National Statistics (ONS) to devise a new measure of well-being.

> "From April next year we will start measuring our progress as a country not just by how our economy is growing, but by how our lives are improving; not just by our standard of living, but by our quality of life."[1]

Beginning in April 2011, the ONS now collect **subjective** well-being estimates to complement existing socio-economic indicators to allow a fuller statistical picture of the nation's well-being. A large sample size is taken which allows for comparisons to be made across regions, genders and ethnic groups. The subjective questions asked are:

· Overall, how satisfied are you with your life nowadays?

· Overall, to what extent do you feel the things you do in your life are worthwhile?

· Overall, how happy did you feel yesterday?

· Overall, how anxious did you feel yesterday?

The first results of this type of survey published in April 2012 were considered by the ONS to be 'experimental', but they had some interesting findings. Women scored more highly than men on the life satisfaction and worthwhile ratings, but scored lower on the anxiety question. Younger and older people scored more highly on the life satisfaction, worthwhile, happiness and anxiety ratings whereas middle aged people tended to score lower in all of these.

## Question

1. The UK experienced unbroken growth from 1992 to 2008. To what extent has this resulted in a higher quality of life for UK citizens?

We turn next to the subject of inequality in incomes.

## ●● Knowledge and Application: Measuring UK income inequality

Before looking at changes in the distribution of income in recent years, let's take a look at how income is distributed across UK households in absolute terms.

As we can see from Figure 4.2, those household incomes at the median level are almost double those at the 10th percentile, and incomes at the 90th percentile are just over double those at the median. At the

---

1. David Cameron, speech on 25th October 2010, http://www.number10.gov.uk/news/britain's-wellbeing-to-be-measured/

*Figure 4.2: Household income at each percentile point in 2010-11 (UK)*

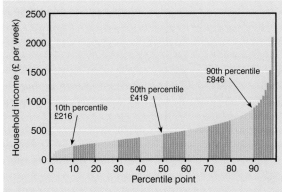

Source: Cribb, Joyce & Phillip, *Living Standards, Inequality and Poverty in the UK 2012*, IFS

top of the distribution there is significant income inequality, with income at the 99th percentile being £2,090 per week, almost two-and-a-half times the income of the 90th percentile.

Changes in income inequality can be measured by looking at changes in the income of quintile groups. The lowest quintile group represents changes in the income of the poorest 20% of households, while the top quintile represents changes in the income of the richest 20% of households. From Figure 4.3 we can clearly see that inequality increased dramatically under the Conservative government of 1979-1997, with the top quintile seeing a much larger rise in income than the bottom quintile. Under the Labour government from 1997-2010 growth in overall inequality was halted. As shown by the data the second quintile experienced the largest rise in income, but all income groups saw incomes rise on average between 1.5% and 1.8% per year, showing little variation between groups.

*Figure 4.3: Real disposable income growth by quintile group, 1979 to 1996/7 and 1996/7 to 2009/10 (before housing costs)*

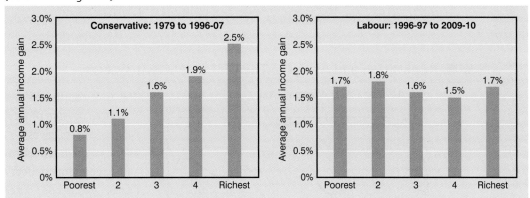

Source: Cribb, Joyce & Phillip, *Living Standards, Inequality and Poverty in the UK 2012*, IFS

*Figure 4.4: Real disposable income growth by quintile group, 2009/10 to 2010/11 (before housing costs)*

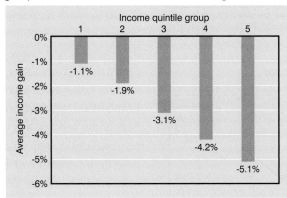

Source: IFS

As previously mentioned real disposable household incomes started falling after the end of the recession in 2009. As shown in Figure 4.4 the incomes of the richest households have been hit harder than the incomes of the poorest households, thus causing a rapid fall in the level of income inequality.

Using quintiles to look at changes in income inequality has its limitations. It hides changes in incomes within quintiles by aggregating them, and changes year-on-year are hidden when looking at patterns over an extended period (as was the case in Figure 4.3). Figure 4.5 looks at changes in income inequality under the Conservatives and Labour at each percentile.

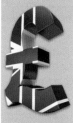

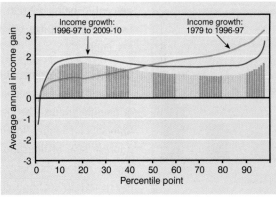

Figure 4.5: Real income growth by percentile point, 1996/7 to 2010/11

Source: IFS

The blue line in Figure 4.5 shows income growth for each percentile under the Conservatives and the red line shows income growth for each percentile under Labour. The difference between the red line and the bars shows the difference between average income growth during the period 1996-97 to 2009-10 and the full period of 1996-97 and 2010-11. The fact that the bars are considerably lower than the red line shows just how significant the recent fall in real disposable incomes has been. Another point of note is how different the fortunes of households within the bottom quintile were under Labour. While households in the second decile (10-20%) in the distribution enjoyed a significant rise in income, the very poorest saw very little rise in household incomes. At the top, those in the 9th decile saw relatively low increases in incomes under Labour compared to other groups, while those at the very top saw very significant increases in household income, particularly the top 1%.

## Question

2. How might economists compare income inequality **between** countries?

## ● ● Application **and** Analysis: **The Gini coefficient system**

Figure 4.6: The Gini coefficient

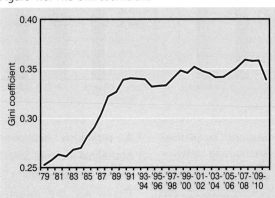

Source: IFS data

Figure 4.7: 90/10 and 99/50 ratios

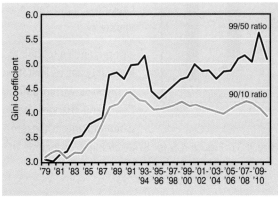

Source: IFS data

The Gini coefficient is a commonly used statistical measure of income inequality. The Gini coefficient gives a number between 0 and 1, where 0 represents perfect equality, and 1 represents perfect inequality (all the income goes to one household). The measure takes into account all of the income distribution.

Another common measure of inequality is the 90/10 ratio. It is simply the ratio of the household at the 90th percentile expressed as a ratio of the household at the 10th percentile. This measure is particularly useful because it compares just two points in the distribution, and therefore ignores fluctuations in the very top and very bottom which can be volatile and may distort the Gini co-efficient measure. The 99/50 ratio is calculated the same way but compares the very top earners to median household income (the 50th percentile).

## ●● Application **and** Analysis: **Recent trends in income inequality and their causes**

Trying to get a comprehensive picture about trends in income inequality is difficult and this is why it is important to use a number of measures as data on *overall* income inequality can mask changes *within* the income distribution. Given the data above, there are a number of conclusions that we can draw about income inequality in the UK. The causes of these changes are also explained.

### 1979-1990: Rising inequality

It is clear from all measures that there was a rapid and widespread increase in income inequality during the 1980s. The Gini coefficient rose from 0.26 to 0.34 during the decade, and Figure 4.3 showed that under the Conservatives the higher level of income, the higher the rate of income growth.

There are several underlying reasons for the rapid rise in inequality during this period:

1. *Technology and demand for skills* – Earnings (or 'original income') inequality grew rapidly. Technological change reduced demand for low skilled workers in a number of industries such as engineering (e.g. computers can do much of the work of clerks). At the same time, advanced technology has made skilled workers who can effectively use the new technology more productive, thus raising their reward through higher wages.

2. *Rapid deindustrialisation* through removing state support for heavy industry reduced the demand for lots of workers in these industries. Structural unemployment affected many, and male participation in the workforce declined, reducing the incomes of these households.

3. The 1980s saw a rapid *rise in female participation* in the workforce. This led to a widening gap between no-earner and two-earner households.

4. Spurred on by government initiatives to encourage entrepreneurship, the number of self-employed workers grew rapidly. As the variation in the earnings of self-employed workers is higher than for all workers, earnings inequality grew overall.

5. In 1981 state benefits became linked to inflation rather than earnings. As earnings tend to rise more quickly than prices those on benefits saw their incomes fall behind the incomes of those in work.

6. Government policies to reduce the power of trade unions meant less wage bargaining power for (usually) relatively low paid workers in many industries.

7. Dramatic cuts in top rates of income tax increased the disposable incomes of those at the top, while the switch to a greater level of indirect taxation reduced the real incomes of those with lower incomes, thus widening inequality.

### 1990-97: Stable, slightly falling inequality

Since 1990 to 1997 inequality remained historically high but fell very slightly overall as shown by the Gini coefficient in Figure 4.6. There are a number of reasons for this:

1. The rapid growth of the mid to late 1980s which caused the earnings of those at the top to pull away from the rest was not prevalent during this period. The early 90s recession and aftermath caused the incomes of higher earners to suffer, as shown by the significant fall in the 99/50 ratio from 1992 to 1995/6.

2. Direct taxation was increased in the early 1990s.

3. Means-tested benefits were introduced in the early 1990s, giving more help to low earners who were in true need of financial help.

*The gap between the 'haves' and 'have nots' increased between 1997 and 2004-5 due to rapidly rising incomes at the top and falling incomes at the bottom.*

### 1997-2004/5: Generally stable overall inequality, convergence for most, divergence at the top and bottom

Under Labour from 1997 to 2004-5 the overall level of inequality remained roughly stable, fluctuating between 0.34 and 0.35. However, the most notable changes during this period were changes within the income distribution. The 99/50 ratio in Figure 4.7 shows that the incomes of the top earners grew much quicker in this period than the median level of household income during this period. However, the 90/10 ratio shows that the income gap between the 90th and 10th percentiles actually fell. At the same time, Figure 4.5 shows that under Labour the bottom percentile were the only group who saw their real disposable income actually fall. So, the gap between the 'haves' and 'have nots' certainly did increase between 1997 and 2004-5, due to rapidly rising incomes at the top and falling incomes at the bottom. Excluding the top and bottom deciles however, income inequality actually fell slightly. There are several reasons why these changes occurred:

1. *The process of globalisation* was rapid and powerful during this period. As UK companies expanded their operations to overseas markets, the actions of top managers could, arguably, raise the value they added to their companies, and thus higher salaries could be justified. Furthermore, in a more globalised economy demand for highly skilled labour including top managers, architects, engineers etc. is very high (just think about the demand for these workers in places like Dubai and Kuwait), and thus the salaries of highly skilled labour grew.

2. The New Labour government limited the number of workers claiming benefits, and incapacity benefit in particular, by *tightening the eligibility criteria for benefits*. In addition the government clamped down on those claiming benefits that they deemed to be capable of work. This caused the income of some at the bottom of the distribution to fall.

3. *Public sector employment* grew dramatically under New Labour (by around 850,000). Moreover, *pay awards for public sector workers exceeded inflation* during this period, and thus the real incomes of a growing number of public sector workers increased considerably, helping many in low paid public sector jobs to catch up with median household income.

4. One of the first pieces of legislation passed by the Labour government was the introduction of *the minimum wage*. The minimum wage increased at faster than the rate of inflation during this period, thus boosting the real incomes of those in work on low pay, and help close the gap with median earnings.

5. The *introduction of tax credits* for working families on low income helped to increase the real disposable incomes of many households.

6. During this period *unemployment fell* considerably, from 2.18 million at the beginning of 1997 to 1.43 million at the beginning of 2005. This fall meant that many at the lower end of the income distribution saw their incomes grow as they gained employment.

7. *National Insurance Contributions* (*NICs*) increased from 2003 which, being broadly progressive, reduced the inequality of disposable household incomes.

**2004/5-2008/9: Rising income inequality**

From 2004-5 to 2008-9 there was a general rise in income inequality, with the Gini coefficient, 90/10 and 99/50 ratios all increasing. This suggests a significant increase in inequality spread across the distribution, although high earners saw particularly strong income growth during this period. This rise in inequality occurred due to:

1. From mid-2005 *unemployment started to rise*, causing a fall in the incomes of those who lost their jobs.

2. From 2004/5 until the beginning of 2008 share *prices and company profits were rising considerably*. Therefore bankers, traders and company bosses increased their pay packets (including bonuses) in line with this, raising incomes at the top end.

3. In 2004 *the EU expanded* to include 10 new member states from Central and Eastern Europe. The UK was one of just 3 of the existing EU members who allowed open access to their labour market for migrant workers. The UK government forecast that around 40,000 migrants would come to the UK from the new EU members, but by the end of the decade around 1 million had arrived. The productive migrant workers were willing to work for relatively little pay, putting downward pressure on wages in mostly unskilled, low paid jobs. Although this helped to control wage inflation in the economy, it hindered the wage growth of relatively unskilled workers in the UK.

**2008/9-2011: A dramatic fall in income inequality or a one off?**

From 2008/9 to 2010-11 a mixed picture emerges. The 90/10 ratio fell throughout this period, suggesting a general fall in inequality. However, the 99/50 ratio increased dramatically between 2008-9 and 2009-10, suggesting rapid income growth for high earners (which is explained below). This explains why the Gini coefficient didn't fall despite the fall in the 90/10 ratio. However, from 2010-11 inequality fell according to all measures, and quite significantly. The Gini coefficient fell from 0.36 to 0.34 in a single year. The fall in income for high earners was a major contributing factor to this fall in inequality. There are several reasons for these changes:

1. The rapid rise in the income of those at the top of the distribution between 2008-9 to 2009-10 was due to high earners bringing income forward (known as 'forestalling') in order to avoid the new 50% income tax rate on income above £150,000 which was introduced by the Labour government and came into effect in April 2010. This meant that although incomes at the top end grew dramatically from 2008-9 to 2009-10, they then fell considerably from 2009-10, causing the Gini coefficient to fall by some way.

2. Real disposable incomes at the bottom rose significantly from 2008-9 to 2010-11 due to rises in tax credits and state benefits faster than the rate of inflation, which came down dramatically due to the recession, with the RPI indicating a period of deflation in 2009.

3. Despite the effects of forestalling in 2009-10, the incomes of those at the top have been hit the hardest by the recession, as shown in Figure 4.4: the higher the level of income, the greater the fall in real

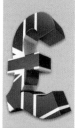

incomes from 2010 onwards. Some estimates suggest that the real incomes of the top 1% have fallen by 15% since the full effects of the financial crisis were felt. The UK economy has a very large financial services sector (roughly 10% of GDP), and workers in this sector tend to have high pay. Since the financial crisis employment in the City of London has fallen by 7%, which has put downward pressure on pay in the sector. In addition poor macroeconomic conditions from 2008 onwards have meant that there is less justification for large bonuses in the financial sector and in the board room as share prices and company profits have struggled. Also, negative media attention and public opinion over 'excessive' executive pay has constrained the pay of top earners. Shareholder revolts have also put a restraint on the increases in pay for company directors.

Perhaps the most notable point to make is not the changes in UK income inequality that have occurred in the last decade, but the **level** of income inequality which is very high by historical standards, and high compared to most other advanced European economies. Many of the underlying causes of rising inequality in the 1980s are still prevalent as reasons for higher levels of inequality in the UK today, and earnings or 'original' income inequality remains high as the labour market rewards highly skilled workers much more than those with few skills.

## ● Knowledge: **The case for and against inequality**

Free market economists argue that inequality is necessary for the efficient functioning of the economy. Workers are paid according to their productivity, and therefore this creates the incentive for workers to work hard. Without the rewards of higher earnings workers would be less productive, and the threat of economic hardship for those who don't work hard makes the economy more productive, encouraging growth and efficiency. Furthermore, free market economists say that inequality is justified as different workers add different levels of value to their employer. If a good CEO performs well and makes decisions which add an extra £300 million to their company's profits, then it is justified for them to be paid more than a secretary at the same company as their value added is considerably less.

Critics of this free market approach argue that inequality is not justified as all workers are part of the wealth creation process, not just the entrepreneurial class. Furthermore, in their book *The Spirit Level* which attracted a great deal of attention when it was published in 2009, Wilkinson and Pickett provided evidence to suggest that societies with greater levels of inequality suffer from more resulting negative externalities such as greater levels of crime, worse public health, and lower social cohesion.[2] However their evidence has been the subject of considerable debate.

### Question

3. Income inequality has been in the spotlight since the 2008 financial crisis and the subsequent recession. To what extent is the UK's current level of inequality damaging for growth and overall social welfare?

There is clear evidence that the overall level of inequality in the UK has not fallen since 1997 despite efforts by the Labour government to redistribute income. The tax and benefit system is redistributive by nature. The incomes of the richest after taxes and benefits are lower than before, and the incomes of the poorest after taxes and benefits are higher. Table 4.3 shows how this occurs.

Direct taxes are taxes which are levied directly on an individual or organisation e.g. income tax. Most direct taxes are **progressive**, meaning that the higher the level of income the greater the proportion of income is taken in tax. Indirect taxes are taxes paid on expenditure on goods and services e.g. VAT, tobacco duty. Indirect taxes are **regressive**, meaning that the higher the level of income the lower the proportion of

---

2. See 'On equality', *The Economist*, 21 August 2010, p. 28.

income is taken in tax. The tax system in the UK overall does little to redistribute income. The benefit system is far more redistributive. Although some cash benefits are **universal** such as the state pension, many are **means-tested** such as income support, and as of 2013, child benefit, which had previously been universal. The change was made as part of the government's deficit reduction strategy.

*Table 4.3: The effects of taxes and benefits on household income*

**Original income** (wages, salaries, self-employment income, pensions, investment income)

| | | |
|---|---|---|
| *add* | Cash Benefits | = **Gross income** |
| *subtract* | Direct taxes and NICs | = **Disposable income** |
| *subtract* | Indirect taxes | = **Post tax income** |
| *add* | Benefits in kind (e.g. NHS) | = **Final income** |

In 2010/11 the top quintile of households had an average original income 16 times greater than the bottom quintile (£81,500 compared to £5,100). After taxes and benefits the average income of the top quintile was just four times greater than that of the bottom quintile (£61,400 compared to £15,200).

## Question

4. Evaluate the view that the best way to redistribute income is through the tax and benefit system.

## Analysis and Evaluation: Government policies to tackle inequality and work poverty

Several policies have been introduced to address inequality and we summarise the key measures.

● The **National Minimum Wage** (**NMW**) – came into effect in 1999 and since then the government have increased the NMW at faster than the rates of both inflation and earnings in most years. For 2012-13 the rate for workers aged 22 and over stands at £6.19, while it stands at £4.98 for 18-20 year olds and £3.68 for 16 and 17 year olds. Supporters of the NMW claim that it reduces poverty and worker exploitation. At the same time it provides a strong incentive for people to work, thus reducing the unemployment and poverty traps.

Critics of the NMW say that despite large differences in living costs between regions, there is no regional variation in the NMW in the UK. In London where the cost of living is highest, there has been a campaign for a London 'Living Wage' which currently stands at £8.30 per hour. This has been supported by some of the main political parties but it is voluntary, and not legally binding. Critics also point out that although the NMW did not appear to cause unemployment during the NICE decade, but during the subsequent recessions when businesses have been less willing to hire workers the NMW could have had a negative impact on employment.

● The **Working and Children's Tax Credits** – Both came into effect in April 2003 to divide the old Working Families Tax Credit into two parts.

The Child Tax Credit can be claimed by people who are responsible for children regardless of whether they are in or out of work. Households on lower income receive a greater amount through the Child Tax Credit system.

The main aim of the Working Tax Credit is to 'make work pay'. Those on low incomes with or without children are able to claim this tax credit. The scheme is designed to improve the incentive to work, thus increasing participation rates and reducing **the poverty trap**. The poverty trap is where a worker, often working part time, has no incentive to work harder or for longer, as this would result in benefits being lost (e.g. free school meals for children) and a greater amount paid in tax. Thus, the very high effective

marginal tax rate discourages work. The Working Tax Credit also reduces **the unemployment trap** by increasing the rewards from work over the income from benefits.

However, the tax credit system is not without its criticisms:

- There will always be a 'withdrawal zone', where benefits are being removed as incomes rise. The existence of this zone provides less of an incentive to work more hours, or take better jobs.

- Tax credits cost the Treasury around £25bn per annum, an enormous cost.

- The system is very complex, and thus there is a large administrative cost associated with the level of bureaucracy. Furthermore, many applying for tax credits complain about the difficulty of the forms that need to be filled in. This complexity has caused the 'take-up rate' for the Working Tax Credit in particular, to be low, at just 61% in 2009/10 according to the HMRC. Furthermore, the complex nature of the system has led to administrative mistakes, with the HMRC overpaying claimants by some £6bn between 2003 and 2007. Fraud has also been a serious problem.

● **The introduction of the 50% top rate of income tax** – In April 2010 a new 50% top rate of income tax was introduced on incomes above £150,000. The Chancellor Alistair Darling introduced the top rate as an 'emergency measure' in his April 2009 budget. It was intended to raise £6bn in tax revenue, as well as reducing income inequality. However, the HMRC estimate that it has raised very little, and Chancellor George Osborne announced in his March 2012 budget that the top rate of income tax would be cut to 45% in April 2013.

● **The New Deal (known as the 'Flexible New Deal' from 2009)** – This programme is aimed at providing training, subsidised employment and voluntary work for the unemployed, thus providing them with the skills necessary to obtain a job in the labour market. Furthermore, the New Deal introduced the ability to withdraw benefits from those who refused 'reasonable employment'.

● **Government funding of apprenticeships** – there has been widespread cross-party support for greater funding of apprenticeships which are seen as a good way of providing people with the skills employers demand and reducing skills shortages in various sectors. However, four out of five companies claim they face barriers to hiring apprentices such as administrative issues and employer's liability insurance.

● **Improving 'in kind' benefits** – the funding of education and healthcare has increased considerably since 1997. Better education and healthcare should help the poorest proportionally more, as it means they should have the level of health and skills that are necessary to be rewarded in the labour market, thus reducing inter-generational poverty.

● **Cutting the basic rate of income tax** – in 2007 Chancellor Gordon Brown cut the basic rate of income tax from 22% to 20%, claiming that this would increase the disposable incomes of many low income families. However, to fund this, he scrapped the lower 10% rate, meaning that many of the poorest families actually saw a fall in their disposable incomes. This drew sharp criticism and the government extended tax credits to try to offset the effects of the tax change.

● **The Winter Fuel Payment and fuel poverty** – The allowance, first introduced in the winter of 1997/98 was aimed at reducing the level of fuel poverty amongst the elderly. Since then however, the payment has been made universal in the sense that it can be claimed by any household with a member over the age of 60. Critics say the measure is very costly for the Treasury, and poorly targeted.

The outlook for income inequality in the UK is uncertain. Despite evidence of pay growth at the top struggling, the Coalition government's planned net tax increases and benefit cuts are forecast to hit low income households the hardest, and thus the fall in income inequality since 2010 may not continue in the future.

## Question

5. Explain the problems of measuring relative poverty and absolute living standards over time.

## ●● Knowledge and Application: **The distribution of wealth in the UK**

Unlike income which is a flow, *wealth is a stock concept*. Household wealth is the total value of assets owned by the household at a point in time. Marketable wealth incorporates physical wealth such as houses, land and cars, as well as financial wealth including financial assets such as shares. Non-marketable wealth (wealth that cannot be sold to anyone else) mainly consists of pension rights. Wealth is usually more unevenly distributed with income, as it is accumulated over a lifetime. Those on higher incomes are able to accumulate wealth through savings, buying shares, getting a mortgage to purchase a house etc. whereas those on lower incomes will struggle to do this. Those with high educational attainment tend to be rewarded in the labour market, and thus wealth and educational achievement are positively correlated.

*Figure 4.8: Distribution (by decile) and sources of wealth in 2006/8 and 2008/10, £m*

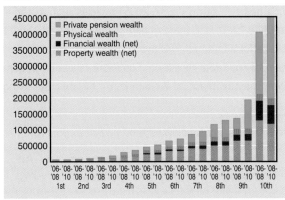

Source: ONS

In addition, wealth increases with age, as it is accumulated during one's working life. Since wealth generates income (e.g. shares pay dividends) wealth inequality is a significant cause of income inequality. Household wealth has increased considerably over the past 25 years, more than doubling between 1987 and 2009, increasing from £56,000 to £117,000 (at 2008/9 prices). Household wealth has fallen slightly since 2007 mostly due to a fall in property prices.

Data for the period 2008-10 shows that the aggregate total household wealth for all households in Great Britain was £10.3 trillion, and the distribution of this wealth is highly uneven. The wealthiest 10% of households were 4.3 times wealthier than the bottom 50% of households combined, and the wealthiest 20% of households owned 62% of total aggregate household wealth. The top 1% own around one-fifth of all household wealth in the UK.

### Extension material: The inheritance tax debate

Inheritance tax is a hotly debated topic. Inheritance tax is levied at 40% on wealth valued at more than £325,000 (in 2012/13) unless it is left to your spouse. The threshold for married couples and civil partners is £650,000. One of the Conservatives key manifesto promises for the 2010 election was to raise the inheritance tax threshold to £1 million. They claimed that passing on your wealth to family members when you die was a natural instinct, and people should have the right to do so. Others, such as the American billionaire investor Warren Buffet are staunch supporters of high inheritance tax. They argue that inheritance tax is one of the few progressive taxes remaining, and it reduces intergenerational wealth and income inequality. Furthermore, allowing people to inherit large amounts of wealth from their parents discourages work and entrepreneurial activity, and some argue that their high standard of living isn't 'earned'. Buffet has warned that the US is in danger of creating an 'oligarchy' if inheritance tax is not increased. When the Coalition government was formed in 2010 the Liberal Democrats had their preferred policy of raising the tax free allowance on income tax implemented, and the inheritance threshold was not raised significantly.

### ● Knowledge: **Poverty definitions**

It is hard to say what exactly 'poverty' means, as people's interpretations as to what constitutes poverty are different. However, economists split poverty into two categories.

**Absolute poverty** is the situation where an individual, household or group struggle to obtain the basic necessities required to sustain human life such as food, water, and clean clothes.

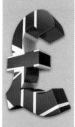

**Relative poverty** is the situation in which an individual, household or group faces a low material standard of living relative to the rest of society, and are in danger of social exclusion. In the UK members of a household are in relative poverty if their household income is less than 60% of the median. This is known as the 'poverty line'.

## ● ● Application and Analysis: **Changes in poverty since 1997**

As income inequality increased between 1979 and 1990 the number of households in relative poverty also rose significantly, with child poverty increasing three fold during this period. Although the early and mid-1990s saw a stabilising or even a slight reversal in child poverty rates, by 1997, the UK's child poverty rate was amongst the worst of all rich nations with around one in three children living in relative poverty. When Labour came to power in 1997 they made a concrete pledge to reduce poverty rates, with a particular focus on child poverty. During Labour's first two terms (1997-2005) policies such as the introduction of the Working Families Tax Credit, the Child Tax Credit, more generous means-tested benefit for pensioners all contributed to a fall in poverty rates for all groups. However, during Labour's third term child and overall poverty rates rose until the onset of the great recession. Since the recession began in 2008 however, relative poverty rates have fallen, but this masks the changes in the absolute living standards of the poorest (as explained below).

*Table 4.4: Relative poverty in the UK: households below 60% of median income (after housing costs, AHC)*

|  | Children (%) | Children (millions) | Pensioners (%) | Pensioners (millions) | All (%) | All (millions) |
|---|---|---|---|---|---|---|
| 1996/7 | 34.1 | 4.3 | 29.1 | 2.9 | 25.3 | 14.0 |
| 2000/01 | 31.1 | 3.9 | 25.9 | 2.6 | 23.1 | 13.0 |
| 2004/5 | 28.4 | 3.6 | 17.6 | 1.9 | 20.5 | 12.1 |
| 2007/8 | 31.1 | 3.9 | 18.1 | 2.0 | 22.5 | 13.5 |
| 2010/11 | 27.3 | 3.6 | 14.2 | 1.7 | 21.3 | 13.0 |

Source: Cribb, Joyce & Phillip Living Standards, Inequality and Poverty in the UK 2012, IFS

*Table 4.5: Relative poverty in the UK: households below 60% of median income (before housing costs, BHC)*

|  | Children (%) | Children (millions) | Pensioners (%) | Pensioners (millions) | All (%) | All (millions) |
|---|---|---|---|---|---|---|
| 1996/7 | 26.7 | 3.4 | 24.6 | 2.4 | 19.4 | 10.8 |
| 2000/01 | 23.3 | 3.0 | 24.8 | 2.5 | 18.4 | 10.4 |
| 2004/5 | 21.3 | 2.7 | 21.3 | 2.3 | 17.0 | 10.0 |
| 2007/8 | 22.5 | 2.9 | 22.7 | 2.5 | 18.3 | 11.0 |
| 2010/11 | 17.5 | 2.3 | 17.5 | 2.0 | 16.1 | 9.8 |

Source: Cribb, Joyce & Phillip Living Standards, Inequality and Poverty in the UK 2012, IFS

From Tables 4.4 and 4.5 the first thing to note is that poverty rates are higher once housing costs are taken into consideration. Labour's policies to tackle poverty were mostly focused on redistributing income towards pensioners and families with children on low income. One criticism of such policies is that working-age non-parents were ignored by policy makers, and poverty rates for this group rose during the period shown above (from 17.2% AHC in 1996/7 to 19.7% in 2010/11). The Labour government set a target in 1999 to halve child poverty by 2010/11, and eliminate it all together by 2020. By 2010/11, child poverty had only fallen from 4.2m to 3.6m (AHC), thus missing the target by some margin.

The Labour government was unsuccessful in meeting overall and child poverty reduction targets despite increasing average spending per child in the social security system significantly. One of the main reasons poverty reduction did not occur is due to the problem with the relative poverty measure. Despite adopting poverty reduction targets the New Labour government had a very relaxed stance on general levels of inequality, and particularly rapid income growth at the top of the distribution. Given that the relative poverty line is measured by 60% of median household income, the only way poverty rates can fall is if incomes at the bottom of the distribution grow quicker than those in the middle. As shown in Figure 4.3 the incomes for all 5 quintiles grew at roughly the same rate under Labour, meaning that relative poverty reduction was difficult as the incomes at the bottom did not gain significantly on those in middle of the distribution. Another contributing factor was the system of state benefits being linked to inflation, which was lower than earnings growth throughout the vast majority of Labour's time in office. Therefore, despite rises in absolute living standards for many of those at the bottom end of the income distribution, relative poverty rates remained stubbornly high.

The effects of the 2008 recession and subsequent squeeze on household incomes caused a fall in relative poverty rates as shown in Tables 4.4 and 4.5. This may seem counter-intuitive at first. As previously mentioned, since the great recession the incomes of those at the bottom of the distribution have been squeezed by less than those at top and the middle of the distribution as shown in Figure 4.4. Therefore, despite falling real incomes across the board, the incomes of the poorest have caught up with the median, thus causing relative poverty rates to fall.

So despite falling living standards at the bottom end of the distribution since the great recession, relative poverty rates have fallen. This highlights a key problem with the measure; it tells us little about absolute living standards. The government have also used measures to look at poverty in absolute terms, by fixing the poverty line at 60% of the 1996/7 median real household income. Using this measure, the IFS estimates that absolute poverty rose by 200,000 to reach 5.8 million (9.6% absolute poverty rate) BHC and by 300,000 to reach 8.4 million (13.8%) AHC in 2010-11.

Another limitation of the relative poverty measure is that it does little to inform us about the living standards of those who are in poverty, and whether their absolute living standards are improving or not. There is some evidence to suggest that relatively the hardship of those in poverty is growing. Despite a general fall in overall poverty rates since 1997, relative poverty using a threshold of 40% of the median has risen.

As planned benefit cuts start to come into full effect the absolute living standards for those at the bottom end of the distribution are set to fall in the next few years. Whether relative poverty rates rise or not depends on how incomes in the middle of the distribution change in coming years.

## Question

6. Evaluate the effectiveness of at least three policies which might be used to reduce inequality and eradicate poverty.

## ● ● Knowledge and Application: An economic divide between regions

Overall data on inequality and poverty in the UK hides substantial inequality between regions. Historically regional policy has been used to help support less prosperous regions but over time the UK has had to adopt a more 'hands off' approach to comply with EU rules and its strong opposition to 'unfair' competition such as state aid. Two remaining initiatives with regional dimensions include:

● The Selective Finance for Investment in England and Scotland program – offers grants to support start-ups, business expansion, innovation and R&D.

● The European Regional Development Fund.

Figure 4.9 shows the considerable variation in weekly earnings between regions, with weekly earnings in London being 35% higher than those in the North East. Also, the data shows something of a North-South divide. The only three regions whose median weekly earnings exceeded that of the UK average were London, East of England and the South-East.

*Figure 4.9: Regional differences in median gross weekly earnings*

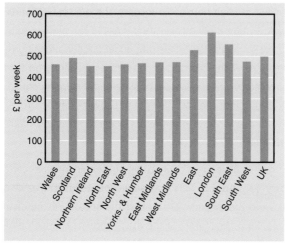

Source: ONS *Region and Country Profile*, 2012

*Figure 4.10: Average house price by country and region in 2012*

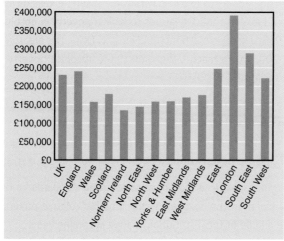

Source: ONS House Price survey

Between 2000 and 2007 many of the less prosperous regions such as the North East started to close the gap as they experienced significant falls in unemployment and rises in house prices. During and after the 2008-09 recession however, Northern Regions suffered more from rising unemployment and house price falls, while property in London and the South-East maintained value better. Further-more, the local economies of several 'outer' regions such as the North-East and Wales have become very dependent upon the public sector. The Coalition's spending and public sector jobs cuts (amounting to 180,000 between 2010 and 2013) have hit those regions the hardest, and the North-South divide appears to be getting larger once again.

Figures 4.9 and 4.10 show much higher levels of earnings and house prices in London than other regions. This has led some economists to point to a London–other regions divide, rather than a North–South divide. However, the London economy is not without its problems. As shown in Table 4.6 unemploy-ment and inactivity rates are above the national average. High house prices have made many dependent upon housing benefit. Obtaining work or more work would mean this important source of income would be lost, creating a large disincentive. Furthermore, the absence of a London minimum wage further reduces the incentive to work. Child poverty is also a major problem in London. The campaign group End Child Poverty estimate that 1 in 4 children in London live in poverty, compared to 1 in 5 nationally. The borough of Tower Hamlets has the highest child poverty level in the UK, at 52%. This highlights a key point of note; there is as much of a divide *within* regions as there is *between* regions.

*Table 4.6: Unemployment and inactivity rates by region*

| | Unemployment rate (%) | Inactivity rates (%) | | Unemployment rate (%) | Inactivity rates (%) |
|---|---|---|---|---|---|
| United Kingdom | 8.3 | 23.3 | East Midlands | 8.0 | 21.9 |
| Wales | 9.3 | 25.3 | West Midlands | 8.9 | 25.5 |
| Scotland | 8.0 | 22.5 | East | 6.9 | 20.2 |
| Northern Ireland | 7.3 | 27.1 | London | 9.7 | 24.7 |
| North East | 11.6 | 26.4 | South East | 6.3 | 20.8 |
| North West | 8.5 | 24.7 | South West | 6.6 | 20.9 |
| Yorks and Humber | 10.3 | 24.6 | | | |

Source: ONS *Region and Country Profile*, 2012

# Chapter 5

# UK Trade, the Current Account and the Value of the Pound

This chapter examines the position of, and recent changes in, the different components of the current account on balance of payments. The significance of the UK's persistent current account deficit is then discussed. Finally, the chapter identifies recent changes in the external value of the pound sterling, the causes of these changes and their importance.

● Knowledge: **The meaning of the current account**

There are three components of the Balance of Payments: The Current Account, the Financial Account and the Capital Account. The most important component of which is the current account balance, which this chapter will focus upon.

In short, the current account measures flows of income into and out of the economy. Each section is itself a 'balance', i.e. it takes into account both inflows and outflows. The current account contains four sections:

1. The **balance of trade in goods**: such as automobiles, pharmaceuticals, agricultural products and oil.

2. The **balance of trade in services**: such as financial services, shipping and tourism.

3. The **income balance**: the balance of factor income i.e. net income from employing factors of production. This could include interest from loans made, dividends from shares purchased, profits from a company's operations, or remittances sent to family members. So, if a UK company makes a profit on an overseas operation, that will cause an inflow of income to the UK thus improving the income balance. If Polish workers in the UK send some of their earnings back to their families in Poland, this represents an outflow of income which will worsen the income balance.

4. **Net transfers** include central government transfers to international organisations such as the IMF, UN and EU, as well as foreign aid.

## Questions

1. What is the different between the budget balance and the current account balance?

2. For each of the following scenarios, identify which section of the current account is affected, and whether an inflow or outflow occurs. Also comment on whether the current account improves or worsens as a result.

   (a) Cars from the Nissan factory in Sunderland are sold to a French car retailer for sale in France.

   (b) The UK government increases its development aid spending.

   (c) Barclays receives repayments (with the agreed rate of interest) from a Swedish company.

   (d) A British manufacturer hires a Dutch company to audit their company accounts.

● Application: **The state of the current account in 2011**

Achieving a surplus on the current account balance was a major macroeconomic policy objective of the UK government for much of the post-war era. Governments believed that in order to buy goods and services from the rest of the world you must export at least as many goods and services or you would be unable to obtain the necessary foreign currency to import without selling off foreign assets, or accumulate excessive levels of debt. From the mid-1980s, however, a combination of the City of London drawing in vast amounts

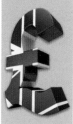

Table 5.1: Summary of the UK current account balance in 2011

|  | £m |
| --- | --- |
| Exports of goods | 298, 987 |
| Imports of goods | 399, 330 |
| Exports of services | 193, 659 |
| Imports of services | 117, 279 |
| Balance of trade in goods and services | -23, 963 |
| Income balance | 171, 535 |
| Net transfers | -22, 216 |
| **Current Account Balance** | **-29, 046** |

Source: ONS, *UK Pink Book 2012*

Figure 5.1: Trade in goods and services

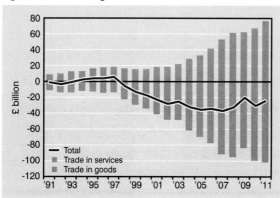

Source: ONS, *UK Pink Book 2012*

Figure 5.2: Top 10 UK export destinations

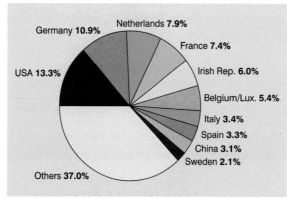

Source: ONS, *Monthly Review of External Trade Statistics*, 2012

Figure 5.3: Top 10 UK import sources

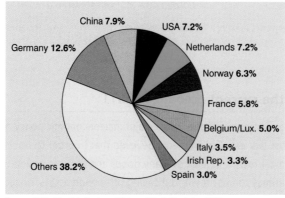

Source: ONS, *Monthly Review of External Trade Statistics*, 2012

of foreign capital, the evolution of a more complex financial system and more relaxed attitude to debt meant that the current account balance became less important as a macroeconomic policy objective. The UK has had a current account deficit every year since 1984. Since the financial crisis of 2008, however, the view that a persistent current account deficit is unsustainable in the long run has become popular once again. Table 5.1 shows that the UK economy has a significant current account deficit, caused primarily by a large trade in goods deficit.

Trade is of vital importance to the UK economy. The UK has a long history of supporting free trade and remains one of the most open advanced economies. The value of exports and imports were slightly above 30% of GDP in 2011. The UK is the world's second largest exporter of services and has run a balance of trade in services surplus since 1966. However, the UK has experienced a prolonged decline in competitiveness for exporting goods, leading to a record trade in goods deficit in 2011 of £100.3bn.

Figure 5.1 shows that over the last 20 years the trade in services surplus has grown while the trade in goods deficit has worsened. For the period shown the trade in goods deficit has worsened more quickly than the trade in services surplus has improved, causing the overall trade balance to fall deeper into deficit.

Despite globalisation, the majority of the UK's trade is done with her neighbours. The EU accounts for 53.2% of the UK's exports, and 49.29% of imports. The amount of trade between the UK and the EU has risen considerably since the UK joined in 1973, but the US, the world's largest economy, remains the largest buyer of UK exports. Most EU countries have experienced sluggish growth in recent years, particularly since the financial crisis of 2008, and subsequent Eurozone debt crisis. This has dashed hopes that depreciation of sterling in 2007 could bring an export-led recovery. Furthermore, most economists agree that the UK needs to re-orient exports towards faster-growing emerging markets,

Figure 5.4: Top 10 UK exports by commodity (£m)

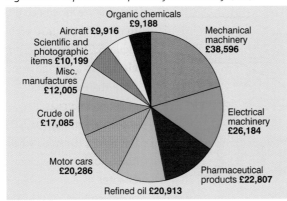

Source: ONS, *Monthly Review of External Trade Statistics*, 2012

Figure 5.5: Top 10 UK imports by commodity (£m)

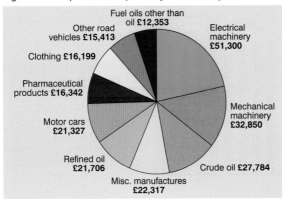

Source: ONS, *Monthly Review of External Trade Statistics*, 2012

Figure 5.6: Trade in goods

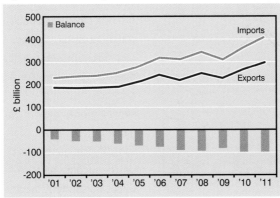

Source: ONS, *UK Pink Book 2012*

Figure 5.7: Trade in oil balance

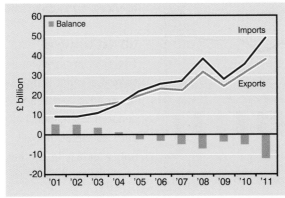

Source: ONS, *UK Pink Book 2012*

as Germany has done. Imports to the UK from emerging economies have risen considerably in recent years, with China now being the second largest source of imports as shown in Figure 5.3. Therefore, most economists agree that the UK needs to rebalance its trade with these economies by exporting more to them.

### (a) The balance of trade in goods

Figures 5.4 and 5.5 show that the UK trades similar items with the rest of the world. The most important traded items for the UK are mechanical machinery, oil (crude and refined), electrical machinery and pharmaceuticals. The UK has traditionally run a trade in goods deficit, and the last 10 years has been no exception, as shown in Figure 5.6. Although the value of exports has grown, the value of imports has risen more than export earnings.

Since the discovery of North Sea oil in the 1980s, net exports of this commodity, as well as natural gas, prevented trade in goods from going further into deficit. Since 2005 however, the UK has run a deficit on its trade in oil balance, as shown in Figure 5.7. The deficit on trade in oil is set to grow as stocks decline over the next decade, with an estimated fall in output of 6% per annum.

### (b) UK balance of trade in services

The UK has run a trade in services surplus every year since 1966. This is mainly because the UK has a **comparative advantage** in services, with financial services playing an especially important role, accounting for around 25% of UK service exports. The English language also makes exports of other professional services such as consultancy and advertising competitive. However, services are not as tradable as goods, and there are greater legal and language barriers for trading services internationally. As a result the value of trade in services is less than that for goods, and the trade in services surplus does not offset the trade in goods deficit, resulting in an overall trade deficit, as shown in Figure 5.1.

A major cause for concern is the UK's high degree of **import penetration**. Import

Figure 5.8: UK balance of trade in services

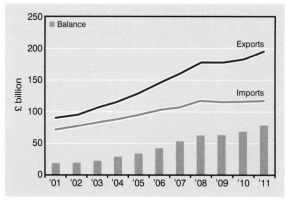

Source: ONS, *UK Pink Book 2012*

Figure 5.9: UK import penetration

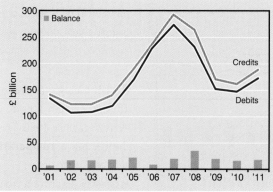

Source: OECD

Figure 5.10: UK net income balance

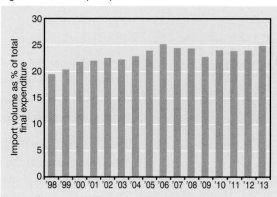

Source: ONS, *UK Pink Book 2012*

Figure 5.11: UK net transfers balance

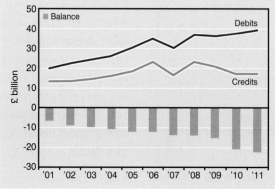

Source: ONS, *UK Pink Book 2012*

volumes into the UK as a percentage of final expenditure have been on a generally upward trend over the last 15 years (as shown in Figure 5.9). UK demand for imports is **income elastic**, so a change in income will result in a more than proportional change in the value of imports purchased. This explains the fall in import penetration in 2009, as recession took full effect. Despite weak or even negative household income growth since 2010 (see Chapter 4), UK import penetration remains significantly higher than the vast majority of the UK's main trading partners. Combined with the relative decline of manufacturing exports it is clear that the UK lacks competitiveness in goods.

## Question

3. Examine two reasons for the UK's relative lack of competitiveness in goods.

### (c) The income balance

The income balance has been in surplus every year since 2001 as shown by Figure 5.10. The growing credits and debits from 2002 to 2007 reflect a strong global economy, causing earnings from investments both in the UK and overseas to grow considerably. The 2008 financial crisis and the subsequent period of slower global growth has caused a fall in earnings from investments inside and outside the UK. The main cause of the UK's surplus on the income balance has been credits on direct investment income exceeding debits every year since 1986, reflecting the strong performance of UK companies operating overseas, particularly financial institutions.

### (d) Net transfers

The final and smallest component of the current account is the net transfer balance. As an advanced economy the UK is a net donor of international aid, and a net contributor to the EU budget. As a result, the UK runs a deficit in the net transfer balance, which has grown in recent years.

## Analysis: **The current account balance during the last decade**

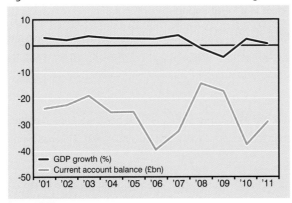

*Figure 5.12: UK current account balance and GDP growth*

Source: HM Treasury

Figure 5.12 shows changes in the current account balance over time. It is clear to see that changes in the current account balance are **counter-cyclical**. That is, when growth rises, the current account balance tends to worsen, and the opposite is true when growth falls. During an upswing or a boom, consumers usually see a rise in their real incomes, and thus they will spend more and some of this increase will be spent on imports. UK consumers have a high marginal propensity to import, and thus this effect will be significant. Furthermore, when the domestic economy is booming firms face capacity constraints, and will tend to focus on the domestic market, thus reducing exports. During a recession, domestic firms tend to focus more on exporting to overseas markets, as domestic sales struggle due to falling real incomes.

Looking more closely within the time period, and accounting for factors other than UK GDP growth, we can identify some clear patterns emerging.

(i)  2001-03: The value of the pound rose between 1997 and 2001, remaining strong during this period (see Figure 5.14 below). Combined with relatively strong domestic growth, but weaker growth globally as the effects of the dot-com bubble bursting were still being felt, the trade in goods balance worsened. However, investment income grew considerably, causing an overall improvement in the current account balance, as shown in Figure 5.12.

(ii)  2004-06: In this period the current account balance worsened considerably. The trade in goods deficit grew, mainly due to the strengthening value of the pound, an increase in credit availability causing a rise in household spending, and the trade in oil balance falling into deficit for the first time in 2005. Furthermore, the income surplus fell from 2005 to 2006.

(iii)  2007-2011: This period was one of recession (2008-9) followed by an anaemic recovery which ended in Q1 of 2012 when the UK officially went back into recession. So although one might expect the trade in goods deficit to improve, this has not occurred. Although the overall current account balance improved considerably in 2007 and 2008, this was due to a rise in the trade in services and income surpluses, rather than a fall in the trade in goods deficit. In 2009, despite a fall in the trade in goods deficit as the recession took full effect, this was more than offset by a fall in the income surplus, causing a slight fall in the current account balance. In 2010, during an upswing the trade in goods deficit increased by £15.7bn, and this was the main driver of the worsening current account position. In 2011 an increase in the trade in services surplus of £9.4bn was responsible for a fall in the overall current account deficit, but the trade in goods deficit worsened once again, reaching over £100bn for the first time (£100.3bn). The trade data at the time of writing in 2012 suggests that the trade in goods deficit has not improved, despite the return to recession.

In summary, despite growth in the trade in services and income balance over the past decade, the current account balance has been in permanent deficit, due to the large trade in goods deficit which has grown considerably. Furthermore despite going through the deepest recession since the 1930s, and the biggest squeeze in household incomes since at least the early 1960s, the UK has continued to run a large current account deficit throughout. This suggests that the UK has a **structural current account deficit** due to a *lack of competitiveness in goods*.

The main reasons for the UK current account deficit are:

● Strong growth in consumer spending during 'the NICE decade' when credit availability was high and the savings ratio was low. This sucked in a lot of imports.

● A strong pound during 'the NICE decade' made UK manufacturing uncompetitive and large parts of the manufacturing sector almost completely disappeared in the UK. This meant that despite a 30% depreciation of the pound (on a trade weighted average) between 2007 and 2008, goods exports did not improve dramatically.

● Growth of the UK's main export partners in the Eurozone had been weak even before the financial crisis of 2008, and many have been in, or returned to, recession since then. This has hindered export growth considerably.

● The UK has experienced high import penetration from globalisation and the industrialisation of developing economies such as China and India.

● Poor non-price competitiveness due to inferior quality or reliability of UK goods.

There are many theories as to why UK firms are less competitive than their rivals in Germany or Japan, the world's second and third largest net exporters (after China). Research shows that UK firm's have, on average, lower productivity and lower levels of investment. This is at least partly due to 'excessive' executive pay. Boardroom remuneration packages are second only to top managers in the US, and up to five times that of top Japanese or German managers. Arguably this crowds-out funds for investment. More importantly, UK companies tend towards the PLC model. Many argue that publicly-owned companies adopt a more short termist approach, favouring cost cutting and short term profit to be distributed as dividends. German and Japanese companies on the other hand tend more towards a privately owned model, such as the German *Mittlestand* (small- to medium-sized usually family-run manufacturing companies), where managers and workers work together more closely to look after the long term interest of the company, and usually invest more in training and capital equipment. Many argue that this approach improves competitiveness in the long run.

## ● Evaluation: **Does the current account deficit matter?**

One's initial reaction is that a current account deficit is a problem. An individual cannot spend more than they earn without running down savings or borrowing. In the same way, an economy cannot buy more from the rest of the world than it sells without borrowing from overseas, or reducing savings and investments abroad. In every year since 1998, the UK has borrowed from abroad to finance its continuing current account deficit. This has resulted in inward investment (UK liabilities) exceeding outward investment (UK assets). However, the City of London has attracted so much direct and portfolio investment over the last 30 years that the UK has received enough financial capital to pay for her current account deficit. However, the financial sector tends to be volatile, and financial companies are highly mobile, especially with strong competition from Shanghai, Dubai and New York, who compete with London as the base for global finance. Many point to the resilience of the City of London, but relying on the financial sector to enable the UK to pay for its current account deficit may not be a sustainable approach.

It is also important to examine how large the current account deficit is as a percentage of total national income, or GDP. If the current

*Figure 5.13: UK current account balance*

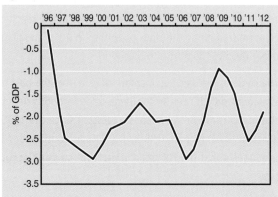

Source: HM Treasury

account deficit is less than 5% of GDP, it is generally thought to be manageable, especially for a relatively creditworthy economy such as the UK. Indeed, many would argue that a current account deficit shows that UK consumers are enjoying a large amount of overseas goods and services, which improve living standards. If the deficit exceeds 5% of GDP, then this is more of a cause for concern. The US has experienced a deficit greater than this several times within the last decade, and the deficits of Portugal and Greece have regularly exceeded 10% of GDP over the last 10 years. *The UK's current account deficit is within manageable limits.*

Although it is hoped the economy will not run a deficit indefinitely, *the large and persistent trade in goods deficit does indicate a structural weakness in the UK economy, particularly in manufacturing.* Since the 2008 financial crisis the

*Relying on the financial sector of the City of London to pay for our current account deficit may not be a sustainable approach.*

major political parties and the Bank of England have repeatedly called for a re-balancing of the economy; away from consumption and imports, towards investment and exports. It was hoped that the fall in consumer spending and rising savings ratio after the financial crisis coupled with a fall in the value of the pound would start this process, but the record trade in goods deficit in 2011 shows that if the re-balancing process does occur, it will take some time. The waning demand for UK exports from struggling Eurozone economies has not helped, but more fundamental changes which increase investment and reduce the *productivity gap* are also needed (see Chapter 6 on this latter topic).

## Questions

4. Explain the causes of the UK trade deficit.

5. Evaluate the view that the UK's current account deficit is a major cause for concern.

## ● Analysis: **The changing value of the pound**

*Figure 5.14: Sterling effective exchange rate index (Jan 2005 = 100)*

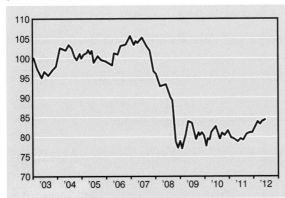

Source: Bank of England

The value of the pound relative to the value of the currencies of the UK's main trading partners is shown in Figure 5.14. The pound operates in a **floating exchange rate** system, meaning the Bank of England does not intervene in setting the value of the pound. The exchange rate is determined by the supply and demand for the pound. The exchange rate appreciated between 1996 and 2001, and then remained broadly constant until 2006, when the value of the pound rose again. The exchange rate fell dramatically, by almost 30% between late 2007 and early 2009. Since then, the pound has gradually appreciated, particularly against the euro.

The reasons for these changes are outlined below:

1996-late 2007: During this period the pound was generally strengthening or remaining at a high level. This was due to:

- Confidence in the UK economic growth and macroeconomic policy framework leading to speculative buying of pounds.

- During this period the Bank of England had higher interest rates than the ECB, Bank of Japan, and at times, the Federal reserve. This led to an inflow of **hot money**.

- The City of London attracted vast inflows of FDI during this period, raising demand for pounds.

- The US trade deficit weakened the dollar, which boosted sterling's trade weighted exchange rate.

Late 2007-mid 2009: The value of the pound plummeted during this period due to:

- A deep recession in the UK reduced confidence in the UK economy, causing speculators to sell pounds.

- The 2008 financial crisis hit the City of London especially hard, halting FDI and portfolio investment flows into the UK.

- Between July 2007 and March 2009 the base rate of interest set by the Bank of England was cut from 5.75% to 0.5%, where it has remained. This caused a hot money outflow.

- A return to a more realistic value against the euro and the dollar was likely to happen sooner or later, and this adjustment occurred as a result of the financial crisis.

Mid 2009-2012: The value of the pound has slowly appreciated due to:

- The pound appreciated against the dollar from a low of £1 = $1.38 in March 2009, but the main reason for the rising value of sterling has been the appreciation of the pound against the euro since 2010, which is given more importance on the trade weighted index as over 50% of the UK's trade is with the eurozone. This has been due to the eurozone debt crisis lowering confidence in eurozone economies. Fears of a currency area break up has caused financial capital to move from the eurozone to the UK, which is seen as a relatively safe haven.

Despite the recent gradual strengthening of the pound since mid 2009, its value remains well below the level experienced at the end of 'the NICE decade'. The consequences of having a weaker pound are:

- An improvement in export competitiveness.

- A decrease in import penetration as the price of imports rises, making domestically-produced goods relatively cheaper.

- A rise in inflation as the cost of essential imports such as food, energy and clothing increase. Also, imported raw material costs rise for domestic firms.

- Potentially, an export-led recovery as foreigners take advantage of cheaper goods and services produced in the UK, and UK consumers reduce the amount they purchase from overseas. However, as mentioned before, there is little evidence such an effect has taken place so far.

- Potentially higher profits for UK companies operating overseas, as their overseas earnings are more valuable in pound terms. This could improve the income surplus.

## Questions

6. Explain what is meant by the term 'Sterling effective exchange rate index (Jan 2005 = 100)'.

7. To what extent will a fall in the value of the pound improve UK macroeconomic performance?

# Chapter 6

# The Supply Side: Productivity and Competitiveness

This chapter examines how the UK economy has performed in terms of productivity growth and why this is an important issue. Measures to raise productivity are considered in the context of diminished competitiveness of UK firms relative to some other developed countries.

## ● ● Knowledge and Application: What is productivity?

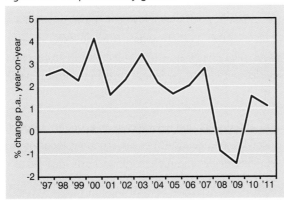

Figure 6.1: UK productivity growth

Source: HM Treasury

**Productivity** measures the ratio of output to input, in other words the production of goods and services as a proportion of the factors of production used to make them. Although productivity can be measured for all factors of production, it is **labour productivity** which is of most concern to macroeconomists. **Labour productivity** is the ratio of output to labour input, typically measured as the total value of output (GDP) per hour worked. Using 'hours worked' rather than the employment level adjusts the data for part-time work and overtime.

Figure 6.1 shows that for much of the period 1997-2007 the UK experienced productivity growth averaging the long-run trend rate of economic growth of 2.5%. However, productivity fell during the recession of 2008-09 and is yet to return to a level above 2%.

## ● Analysis: What drives increases in productivity?

Productivity growth is a key measure of macroeconomic performance. It refers to the increase over time in the productive capacity of the macroeconomy and, therefore, drives long-run, or trend growth. We can identify a number of the determinants of labour productivity:

### 1. Investment in human capital

Highly-skilled and trained workers are more productive as they can produce more output in a given period of time, with less waste. Better management can also motivate workers to be more productive, and organise resources better so workers can focus on core performance. Education and training are fundamentally important in creating workers with relevant and transferable skills, and good healthcare can also boost labour productivity by keeping workers healthy and reducing the number of working days lost to illness.

### 2. Investment in physical capital

Fixed capital investment – spending by firms on ICT and up-to-date technologies and machinery – boosts labour productivity in two ways. Firstly, it allows some replacement of labour by capital in tasks where a machine or robot is more efficient and accurate, for example in some manufacturing tasks such as car production. Secondly, better equipment can increase the productivity of remaining workers by allowing them to better organise their time or to perform manufacturing tasks.

### 3. Financial capital

If investment drives productivity gains, it is crucial that firms of all sizes have access to affordable credit. This allows them to invest in the latest technologies and match competition in both domestic and

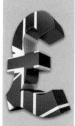

international markets. The credit crisis in 2007 and its lasting impact on capital markets can be seen as one cause of the UK's 'productivity gap' (see later in the chapter).

### 4. Product market competition

The more firms there are competing in a market, the more likely they are forced to compete on both prices and costs. Labour costs contribute a significant proportion to total costs in most modern organisations, and therefore firms will work hard to keep unit labour costs as low as possible. The key here is labour productivity: highly-skilled workers are valuable even if their wages are higher than other workers, as their higher cost is offset (and probably outweighed) by their increased output levels.

### 5. Labour market competition

The negotiating power of workers is an important determinant of labour productivity. Where workers enjoy considerable bargaining power (for example when unemployment is low, or when a worker has skills in shortage in the labour market) they can push up their wages. This will increase their employer's labour costs. Similarly, in an economy where trade unions are strong there may be lower productivity levels, and policies such as minimum wage legislation can increase labour costs in the lowest-paid jobs.

### 6. Infrastructure

Infrastructure refers to the transport and distribution networks in an economy. Good infrastructure eases the flow of workers, raw materials and finished goods across the economy, reducing the labour hours lost to unpredictable commuting travel times, delays and fuel and driver costs incurred as output is delivered to markets. Both internal and external transport links are crucial in keeping distribution costs to a minimum, and in making the UK an attractive place to do business and attract foreign direct investment.

### 7. Government policies

Many of the factors already raised can be influenced by government intervention (or lack of intervention) in the markets for raw materials, financial capital, labour and transport. Research and development (R&D) spending can also be targeted through the use of tax breaks and subsidies.

● Analysis: **Why is productivity growth important?**

Productivity growth is important for a number of reasons:

1. Productivity growth improves living standards by increasing the level of output relative to the size of the population. This helps to explain why real incomes and real output tend to increase over time, and why each generation enjoys a wider and more affordable range of goods and services than the generation before. Productivity gains boost output per worker, and also reflect the adoption of new innovations and inventions which increase quality of life as well as standard of living.

2. Increases in productivity increase output through supply-side improvements, rather than higher aggregate demand. As long-run aggregate supply rises, output and employment levels rise without pushing up prices; indeed, the price of some goods and services may fall as their unit costs fall. Non-inflationary growth does not carry the same trade-off between output and inflationary pressures, and thus is seen as highly beneficial for (nearly) all economic agents.

3. Labour productivity is a key factor in determining international competitiveness: the ability of an economy such as the UK to produce the goods and services demanded by global consumers, firms and governments. **Unit labour costs** are a key performance measure, and are calculated by dividing average wages by average output. If the UK is able to compete strongly in international markets it will experience demand for its exports. This will avoid problems with current account imbalance and create jobs for UK-based workers and profits for UK-based firms, rather than those in other countries.

4. Finally, productivity growth can be a sign of other strengths. If labour costs are low relative to output, this can reflect an economy with well-trained, organised and motivated workers. High levels of

investment create both demand and future supply, and the incomes and profits created by economic activity will boost government's tax receipts. A strong infrastructure improves quality of life as well as keeping firms' costs low.

There are possible drawbacks to strong labour productivity growth, the main one being **structural unemployment**. This exists when the unemployed (those *seeking work*) do not have the relevant skills for the vacancies available (the firms *seeking workers*). Structural unemployment is often linked closely to shifts in technology and patterns of global production, and is most likely where workers have specific and non-transferable skills related to industries which move overseas to take advantage of cheaper labour and land (see Chapter 7).

## Question

1. Paul Krugman has said that "productivity isn't everything, but in the long run it is almost everything."[1] Why is it arguable that productivity growth is, in the ultimate, the key indicator of a country's standard of living?

## ● Application: **UK versus global productivity performance**

*Figure 6.2: Average productivity growth for selected G7 members, 1997-2007 and 1997-2011*

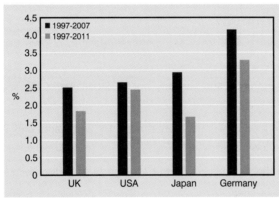

Source: HM Treasury

*Figure 6.3: Highest annual increase in productivity, 1997-2007*

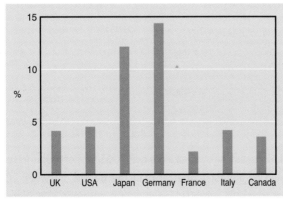

Source: HM Treasury

Figure 6.2 shows how average UK productivity growth compared with other major economies over two time periods. For the period 1997-2007 the UK experienced a growing gap in productivity against the USA, Japan and Germany. A similar trend is shown for 1997-2011, where a dramatic fall in productivity in 2009 (-14.8%) dragged down the Japan average. For the G7 economies, the highest annual increase in productivity recorded since 1997 is shown in Figure 6.3. Even in its best year the UK did not perform well compared with several other developed economies.

As seen in Figure 6.4, the UK and USA have invested a lower proportion of GDP than Germany and Japan in recent years, and their productivity growth has been lower as a result. However, other economies such as France and Italy have also suffered low productivity growth despite proportionately higher levels of investment.

---

1. P. Krugman, *The Age of Diminished Expectations*, 1999.

Figure 6.4: Investment as % of GDP (2001-2011 average) for G7 economies

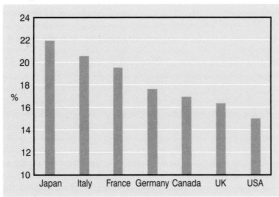

Source: HM Treasury

**Question**

2. Figure 6.4 shows that Italy and Japan both devoted over 20% of their GDP to investment but in Figure 6.3 the two countries differed in their experience in productivity growth. How could one explain this difference?

## ● Analysis: **The UK productivity gap**

The term 'productivity gap' has been used in recent years to describe the loss of competitiveness of UK firms against those in similar economies. It is a key factor in the debate surrounding deindustrialisation (see Chapter 3, and Figure 3.3 in particular) and is often given as a cause of the relatively low rate of trend economic growth experienced in the UK.

A study by the London School of Economics' Centre for Economic Performance[2] identified the following key aspects of the UK productivity gap:

● Output per hour worked was almost 40% lower than in the USA and 20% lower than in Germany and France.

● Output per worker was similar in the UK and Germany, but UK labour works 16% higher hours than in Germany.

● The key factors explaining the productivity gap between the UK and France and Germany are lower capital invested per worker and lower skills.

● The productivity gap between the UK and USA is most acute in three sectors: wholesale and retailing, hotels and restaurants, and financial services.

● The productivity gap between the UK and USA was caused less by a lack of investment in labour and capital, and more by differences in managerial methods and technology.

Since 2004, the productivity gap has remained.

Table 6.1: Changes in UK productivity, 2003-2012

| | |
|---|---|
| Output per worker | 7.3% |
| Output per job | 7.4% |
| Output per hour | 9.4% |
| Unit labour costs | 22.9% |

Source: ONS

Table 6.1 shows how although UK output has increased since 2003, in particular in terms of output per hour, unit labour costs have risen by almost a quarter over the period. Between 2006 and 2010 the UK-USA productivity gap increased by 9%, with US productivity per hour 23% higher than in the UK. Similar gaps of 18% and 16% were recorded between the UK and Germany and France respectively. Figure 6.5 compares growth in unit labour costs with other G7 economies and the eurozone average.

2. http://www2.lse.ac.uk/newsAndMedia/news/archives/2004/UKs_ProductivityGap.aspx

*Figure 6.5: Average growth in unit labour costs, 1993-2011 and 2001-2011*

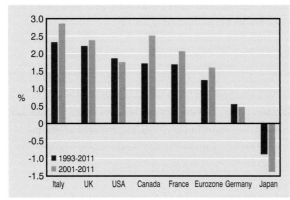

Source: HM Treasury

*Figure 6.6: Sterling effective exchange rate index (January 2005 = 100)*

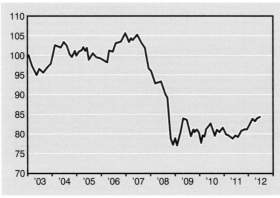

Source: Bank of England

The UK and Italy clearly saw unit labour costs in their manufacturing sectors increase by more than the G7 and eurozone averages. In comparison, Japan saw its labour costs fall over both periods, and Germany enjoyed wage inflation of less than 1% compared to output levels.

It should be noted that this data reflects the strength of domestic currencies, or in the case of Germany, Italy and France, the strength of the euro. A stronger, or appreciating currency increases the prices of domestically-produced goods and services in overseas markets; a depreciating currency reduces the prices of domestic outputs overseas.

The relatively strong pound during 'the NICE decade' therefore could go some way in explaining comparatively poor unit labour costs, but would not explain the 'real' gap in output per hour and output per worker. Figure 6.6 shows the sterling effective exchange rate index between 2003 and 2012. This is a trade-weighted average, and therefore reflects the relative importance of different currencies. Throughout 2003 to 2008, the index remained high, but the fall in sterling throughout 2008 should have increased UK productivity relative to other major trading partners.

## ● Analysis: **The 'productivity puzzle' in 2012**

The trends in employment, unemployment and productivity levels in the UK in recent months has given rise to the term 'productivity puzzle.' With output contracting (falling real GDP in the double dip recession), economists would expect to see unemployment rising and employment falling. However, in the final months of 2012 the UK saw rising employment and falling unemployment. The impact of this on UK productivity is clear: more workers producing fewer goods and services implies a fall in output per worker. This is explored further in Chapter 7, where the main causes suggested are 'labour hoarding', a collapse in investment, and falling real wages.

### Questions

3. Why would you expect labour hoarding by employers to have an adverse effect on productivity?

4. If interest rates are very low why nonetheless might employers be reluctant to install new capital equipment?

## ● ● Analysis **and Evaluation: Minding the gap – policies to boost productivity**

The causes of productivity growth were explored earlier in this chapter, and possible policies to increase productivity performance will therefore be closely linked to these.

### 1. Investing in human capital

Recent governments have stressed, in different ways, the importance of creating an efficient, competitive workforce with the skills and abilities necessary for the UK to compete in increasingly globalised product markets. A key debate is to what extent skills can and should be developed through private firms and free markets, or by government. The relative importance of vocational and academic skills is also open to argument. Immigration is one way of bringing higher skilled workers into the UK labour market, but this can also lead to higher unemployment even if employment is rising.

### 2. Investing in physical capital – the importance of financial capital

Trends in investment spending are covered in greater detail in Chapter 3, but a key determinant is the cost and availability of finance. Again, the debate hinges on whether greater government intervention will increase or decrease the cost of loans to firms. Banks were criticised during the credit crisis for easy lending during the NICE decade, and are now criticised for tightening the terms of their lending as the economy struggles to recover from recession.

In addition, the reward for research, development and investment is important: high rates of corporation tax can limit the incentive for firms to expand and adopt new technologies, as well as reducing post-tax profits which are used by some firms as a source of finance.

Free market economists argue that bureaucracy also increases unit costs and limits innovation by raising the cost of doing business in the UK. They would also argue that, in terms of research, governments have a habit of 'backing losers' and subsidies to potential innovators create a culture of state dependency with low incentives for success.

### 3. Increasing product market competition

This is seen by many economists as the key driver of innovation, investment and rising productivity. Globalisation and free trade expose UK firms to powerful market trends, forcing them to control their costs to compete. However, this has also led to the loss of jobs to overseas producers and production plants, with structural unemployment resulting in the UK.

### 4. Increasing labour market competition

The 'labour hoarding' argument given for the productivity puzzle suggests that UK labour markets may not be as flexible as expected. If firms are holding on to workers despite falling demand, this suggests the costs of redundancy are high and there may be a shortage of sufficiently skilled workers when the economy recovers.

Labour market imperfections such as the National Minimum Wage may also raise labour costs and reduce productivity, but such initiatives play an important role in creating social welfare and reducing poverty and inequality.

*Large scale investment projects such as new runways can boost both short- and long-run growth.*

## 5. Investing in infrastructure

Large scale investment projects such as new runways (or even airports) and spending on public transport can boost both short-run growth (through Keynesian-style expansion and related multiplier and accelerator effects) and long-run growth (through reducing transport costs and increasing production and distribution potential).

The UK road, rail and airport network is seriously congested, particularly around major population areas such as London and the north-west conurbation of Manchester and Liverpool.

However, public spending is currently limited by the Coalition government's austerity measures, which aim to bring down public spending as a proportion of GDP to allow greater free market activity.

At least until 2015 (and possibly later given the Labour Party's agreement on the need to cut the budget deficit, albeit over a slightly longer time scale) it appears unlikely that the UK will see a1930s-style public spending stimulus in an attempt to boost growth, create jobs and ultimately raise productivity.

## ●● Knowledge and Application: **UK mergers and competition policy**

The competitiveness of UK industry is often referred to as a determinant of external trade performance on measures such as the current account of the balance of payments. However, competitiveness within the UK, and within particular sectors of the economy, is an important influence on productivity.

Conventional economic theory emphasises the importance of competition. Firms enjoying monopoly power (in markets where there is *imperfect competition*) can charge high prices, lack an incentive to innovate, and produce goods inefficiently. However if firms are forced to compete aggressively they will be forced to innovate to gain competitive advantage or even just to survive, and will produce goods efficiently.

In the UK the Department for Business Innovation and Skills (BIS) has responsibility for ensuring UK firms and markets are competitive. This has both microeconomic and macroeconomic benefits:

> *"Competitive markets provide the best means of ensuring that the economy's resources are put to their best use by encouraging enterprise and efficiency, and widening choice."*[3]

The two key issues are whether the actions of firms **lessens competition** or leads to an abuse **of market power** (or monopoly power).

UK competition policy is set by the Secretary of State for Business Innovation and Skills and enforced through four competition bodies:

● The **Office for Fair Trading** (**OFT**) investigates potential mergers and anti-competitive practices (such as price fixing or the forming of collusive cartels).

● The **Competition Commission** (**CC**) conducts more detailed investigations into merger activity, market behaviour and the workings of industry regulators such as OFCOM and OFGEM.

● The **Competition Appeal Tribunal** (**CAT**) is a judicial body which rules on appeals related to decisions made by the competition authorities.

● The **European Commission** rules on large-scale mergers with a European dimension and can investigate anti-competitive practices within the EU and European Economic Area (EEA: EU plus Iceland, Liechtenstein and Norway).

The government plans to reform the OFT and CC to form a single body, the Competition and Markets Authority (CMA) in 2014. In addition, specific sectors are controlled by sectoral regulators such as energy markets (OFGEM: Office for the Gas and Electricity Markets), water suppliers (OFWAT), the communications sector (OFCOM), railway services (ORR), air traffic services (CAA) and the NHS (Monitor).

---

3. http://www.bis.gov.uk/policies/business-law/competition

Firms see takeover bids as one way of increasing productivity. Cost savings, or economies of scale, can be made by combining head office functions such as finance, marketing and human resources, and also by sharing market and technical knowledge and technology. However, the impact of merger activity can harm consumers and suppliers if the larger, combined firm can abuse its monopoly and monopsony power. In addition, cost-cutting can result in higher unemployment and higher levels of indebtedness in the firm (particularly where it has been funded through private equity activity). Any merger which will result in a firm having a market share greater than 25% is investigated by the OFT and where an unacceptable lessening of competition or a threat of abuse of market power is predicted, the case is currently referred to the CC.

Recent developments in competition policy in the UK include:

- The OFT can refer any potential merger to the CC without requiring Secretary of State approval.

- The Secretary of State now has a reduced role and can only intervene where there is very strong public interest or where turnover is greater than £70 million.

- A more similar system to the USA, where the key test is whether there is a 'substantial lessening of competition'.

- The criminalisation of cartels; the maximum sentence is five years in prison for a guilty company director.

- Parties have the right to appeal to the CAT for a statutory judicial review of any decision made by the OFT or CC.

In summary, these changes have attempted to depersonalise and depoliticise the operation of UK competition policy, removing Ministerial decision-making as far as possible and to encourage firms to engage in fair, competitive activities to the benefit of all economic agents.

One case of recent interest was the takeover of Halifax Bank of Scotland (HBOS) by Lloyds Bank in 2008. This was a case of a merger which clearly resulted in the lessening of competition in the market for residential mortgages, but which was allowed by the UK government as the potential collapse of HBOS (fuelled by rumours of imminent bankruptcy, requests for emergency funding from the Bank of England, and exposure to bad debts stemming from the subprime crisis) was seen as potentially catastrophic for the wider UK banking sector. The impact of the high level of market power enjoyed by Lloyds as a result of the approval of this merger was investigated as part of a report published in 2011 as part of a possible break-up of large banks in the UK. The merger has affected Lloyds Bank adversely, with HBOS carrying much higher levels of bad debt than expected. Some critics argued that nationalisation of HBOS would have been a more effective policy than allowing the merger with Lloyds to take place.

## Questions

5. Explain how, since the 2002 Enterprise Act, competition policy in the UK is now much less the subject of Ministerial intervention and thus compared with earlier years has now become depoliticised.

6. Why is competition policy relevant to concern over the growth of productivity?

# Chapter 7

# Employment and Unemployment

This chapter compares two measures of the number of people out of work in the UK before examining what factors account for changes in the numbers of unemployed. The final section considers the relationship between unemployment and the rate of inflation.

## ● Knowledge: **Defining unemployment**

**Unemployment** describes the status of people who are willing, able and available for work at current wage rates who cannot find a job. The total number of workers (including both those in work and those who are not) in an economy is called the **workforce**. Unemployment can be expressed as either a level (e.g. 3 million unemployed) or as a percentage of the workforce (e.g. 10% unemployment). Economists also distinguish between people who are **economically active** and **economically inactive**. The **economically active** are those of working age (16 and over, and below the retirement age) who are in employment or are unemployed.

The **economically inactive** are those of working age who are neither employed nor unemployed, and include:

- Students in full-time education (including school, college and university students).
- Workers who have taken early retirement.
- People too ill or infirm to work.
- People who have given up searching for work or not currently seeking work (e.g. university or school leavers waiting to take up a job offer).

A contentious issue in economics is that of **full employment**. From 1945 until the 1970s, the UK government expressed a clear policy of aiming to create as high employment as possible, thereby minimising unemployment. Later in the chapter we will discuss how different economists may define 'full employment' in different ways. Indeed, some Conservative governments since the 1970s have stressed the importance of price stability (carefully controlled inflation) compared with achieving full employment.

## ● Application: **Measuring unemployment**

Unemployment is measured in two different ways in the UK.

1. The **claimant count (CC)** measures unemployment as **the total number of people out of working and claiming Jobseeker's Allowance (JSA)**.

   It can be argued that the claimant count understates unemployment, as some people may be out of work but not claiming benefits for reasons such as:

   - The individual's savings are too high to make them eligible for JSA (many welfare state benefits are means-tested to some extent).
   - Household income may be relatively high if a partner or family member is economically active.
   - Some people are ineligible for JSA, for example those who have not built up sufficient National Insurance contributions in the past, or those who are not EU citizens.
   - People who have left their previous job voluntarily or been dismissed for misconduct are ineligible for JSA.
   - Some people may be too embarrassed to claim benefit, or do not understand that they may do so.

It is important to note that where benefit is claimed fraudulently this will increase 'unemployment' on the claimant count measure.

2. The **Labour Force Survey (LFS)** measures unemployment by conducting **a sample survey of over 60,000 households (and over 100,000 people) every three months**. This is the government's official preferred measure of unemployment and compares directly to data collected from all countries according to the International Labour Organisation (ILO). The LFS measure therefore allows economists to judge UK economic performance in the labour market against other economies.

The LFS categorises an individual as unemployed if they:

● Out of work.

● Actively seeking work.

● Been looking for work in the past four weeks.

● Are able to start work within two weeks.

## ● Application: **UK unemployment data**

Figure 7.1: Labour Force Survey and Claimant Count unemployment, UK

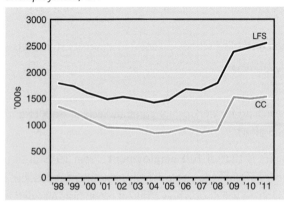

Source: HM Treasury

Figure 7.2: Labour Force Survey and Claimant Count unemployment, UK

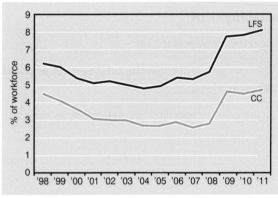

Source: HM Treasury

Figures 7.1 and 7.2 show the unemployment story for the UK economy over the past 15 years. Figure 7.1 compares Claimant Count and Labour Force Survey levels of unemployment; Figure 7.2 compares the rates of unemployment.

## ● Analysis: **Why do the two measures of unemployment differ so much?**

The claimant count is consistently below the Labour Force Survey measure, supporting the view that the former understates unemployment. However, the differential between the measures varies, as shown in Figure 7.3, where data prior to 1998 has also been included to allow for more detailed analysis.

It is very evident that the difference between the LFS and the Claimant Count has increased over the period shown. Possible explanations for the growing divergence between the two measures are:

● Increasing benefit ineligibility (see section on Measuring Unemployment above).

● The impact of long-term unemployment on job seeking; workers who remain jobless for a long period of time may become discouraged to search any longer, or reach retirement age, and therefore stop actively seeking work.

*Figure 7.3: Differential between Labour Force Survey and Claimant Count measures (LFS-CC)*

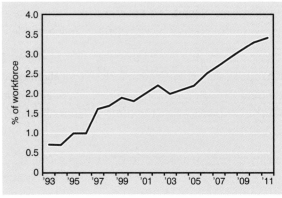

Source: HM Treasury

*Figure 7.4: Claimant Count as a percentage of Labour Force Survey, UK*

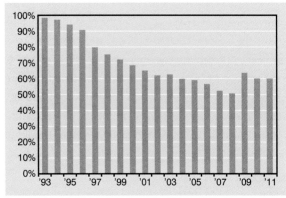

Source: HM Treasury

- The LFS measures members of households who may not be actively seeking work but would accept a job if available, for example parents considering a return to the workforce after taking time to raise a family.

- The stigma associated with 'benefits culture' may prevent some groups such as early retirees from claiming benefits even though they might like to find full-time work in another career or on a part-time basis to supplement income from pensions.

- Increased unemployment of higher earners (perhaps linked to increased incomes in general) which allows workers who have been made redundant to survive on savings and termination packages whilst they look for work.

Figure 7.4 shows how the CC consistently fell relative to the LFS measure between 1993 and 2008, followed by a sharp uplift during and after the recession of 2008-09. It can be argued that, during a recession, the Claimant Count increases because as major earners are made redundant, other possible earners will also become eligible for benefits.

## ● Analysis: **Causes of unemployment in the UK economy**

The relationship between unemployment and economic growth is important. Both demand and supply-side factors influence the rates of job creation and job destruction across the economy. It should be noted that new employment opportunities arise even during periods of local and national decline, and there may be job losses and even the collapse of some sectors even when the economy is experiencing a boom.

The difference between those jobs created and those lost will therefore determine the net impact on unemployment in a region or across the United Kingdom.

A key issue in labour markets in rapidly evolving and changing economies is that of the mismatch between the skills of workers losing their jobs and those needed to be successful in finding work in sectors and roles where there are vacancies.

As seen on Figures 7.1, 7.2 and 7.3, UK unemployment has varied widely even over the relatively short period of the past 20 years. Those years can be divided into the following periods:

### 1993-2004: Stable economic growth

Unemployment fell consistently over this period, with the Labour Force Survey measure in 2004 at less than half of that recorded in 1993 as the economy began its recovery from recession.

The major downward driver of unemployment was, of course, strong and stable economic growth. The departure of sterling from the Exchange Rate Mechanism in 1992 effectively devalued the pound by around 15% against the other major European economies, allowing an export-led boom to create demand

for UK goods abroad, in turn creating jobs for UK-based workers. By 1997 the UK had entered the 'NICE decade', where globalisation, high business and consumer confidence buoyed by positive wealth effects arising from housing market and stock market booms, and a powerful new faith in the abilities of the fiscal and monetary authorities created a low inflation, high growth platform for job creation.

Another important factor, this time on the supply-side of the economy, was the introduction of labour market policies aimed at creating increasing job opportunities. The New Labour government elected in 1997 quickly introduced the **New Deal** in 1998, a 'welfare to work' or 'workfare' programme designed to increase employability in groups such as unemployed youths, the long-term unemployed, lone parents and the disabled.

The New Deal introduced the ability to remove benefits from people unwilling to take up 'reasonable employment'. After 6 months, for example, all 18-24 year olds claiming Job Seeker's Allowance were expected to take up a subsidised work placement, a place in full-time education or training, or participate in either the Community Task Force or the Environmental Task Force (both designed to put spare labour to use in the local community or voluntary sector, at the same time as giving skills and experience to the young jobless).

In addition to making benefits more conditional, policies such as the National Minimum Wage (1999) and Working Families and Children's Tax Credits (1999, amended 2003) were designed to reward employment through higher pay and lower tax payments respectively. An important consideration for the unemployed is the **replacement ratio: the difference between earned and unearned income**. For lower-skilled workers, generous benefits payments may make taking up a job opportunity irrational, once taxes, travel, equipment and clothing and possibly the costs of childcare are taken into account. By increasing the replacement ratio, a greater incentive to work is created and unemployment should fall (providing there are sufficient opportunities for employment).

Other trends contributed to the *flexibility of the UK workforce.* Growth in part-time employment through the 1990s and beyond, typically but not exclusively for working parents, helped to reduce unemployment, as did the greater wage flexibility provided by the erosion of trade unions powers throughout the 1980s. Greater education, training and retraining opportunities help workers to develop, maintain and adapt their skills to the demands of the modern workplace and reduce their susceptibility to structural changes and resulting unemployment.

The New Labour government of 1997 quickly gave independence to the Bank of England to set the base rate of interest at a level which suited the economy rather than the government (see Chapter 9). The Chancellor, Gordon Brown, also introduced fiscal rules (see Chapter 10) to hopefully constrain the government from using government spending and taxation policies to create an artificial boom which would boost their popularity and make them more electable. It could be argued that the high degree of faith in demand management policies to set the economy on a firm footing increased investment (both domestically and from overseas) which led to private sector expansion, which created jobs.

*Figure 7.5: Change in employment levels, public and private sector*

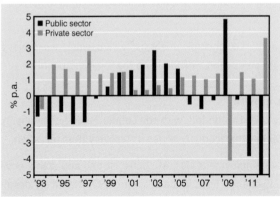

SourceL ONS

The *growth of the public sector*, and public sector employment was a key characteristic of the New Labour years. Figure 7.5 shows the change in public sector and private sector employment between 1992 and 2012.

Between 2001 and 2005, public sector employment rose significantly faster than the private sector. However, in terms of total

Figure 7.6: Total employment by sector in the UK
(public versus private)

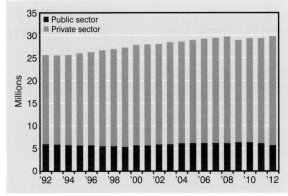

SourceL ONS

Figure 7.7: UK Youth Claimant Count unemployment
(000s, 18-24 year olds, 6 months+)

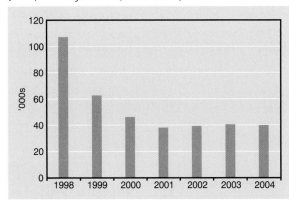

SourceL HM Treasury

Figure 7.8: Annual % change in real GDP and
unemployment (Claimant Count)

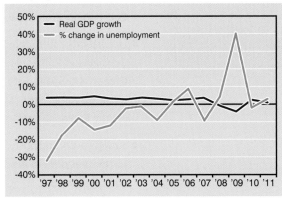

SourceL HM Treasury

employment, it should be noted that the private sector remained – and remains – the major employer in the UK economy (see Figure 7.6).

Demographic and education sector trends also played a part in reducing unemployment. With a decline in the birth rate since the late 1960s, and increasing numbers of 16-24 years olds taking up places in further and higher education, youth unemployment declined dramatically during this period.

### 2005-2009: Slowdown in growth

The key contributor to employment and unemployment figures in the period 2005 to 2009 was the slowdown in economic growth experienced by the UK economy. Figure 7.8 shows this important relationship between real GDP growth and change in unemployment.

As the economy grew throughout the first half of the NICE decade there was a continuous fall in unemployment. However, as growth dropped below the trend rate in 2005 unemployment began to rise, with a predictably dramatic rise experienced in 2009 before the economy moved out of recession in 2010. The data for particular sectors of the labour market provides a more detailed picture of how recession affected certain workers. Figure 7.9 shows the impact of slowdown and recession on the long-term and youth unemployed.

Both measures more than doubled between 2008 and 2010, and the impact on youth unemployment in particular has been covered widely in the press. The phenomenon of the 'NEETs': **16-24 year olds not in employment, education or training** is of great concern and could create a 'mini-generation' of young people facing atrophied skills and a lack of experience in the workplace. It is possible that, even if the economy recovers relatively quickly, this current cohort of NEETs will be passed over for new jobs as new school and university leavers enter the labour market.

Figure 7.9: Long-term (25 years old +, >12 months unemployment) and Youth (18-24, >6 months unemployment) unemployment in the UK

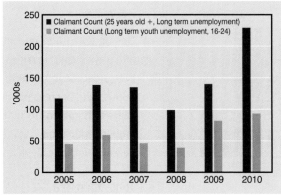

SourceL HM Treasury

**Question**

1. How does the data in Figures 7.7 and 7.9 illustrate the concern over the phenomenon of the Neets?

## 2009 onwards

Figure 7.10 shows how UK unemployment rose throughout the recession of 2008-09, albeit with a time lag of a few months. Between mid-2008 and mid-2009, the LFS measure recorded an increase in joblessness of 1 million. Even when the economy returned to slow growth in 2010, unemployment remained high around the 2.6 million level. In 2012, the UK economy returned to recession. It is clear that the main cause of joblessness now in the UK remains demand-deficient unemployment. Several factors have contributed to a fragile labour market where employers are reluctant to create sufficient new jobs to replace those destroyed in the recent recession:

Figure 7.10: Labour Force Survey Unemployment, UK (monthly data, millions)

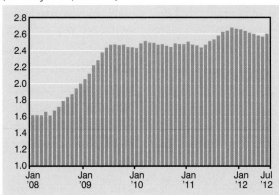

SourceL ONS

Figure 7.11: Business optimism (British Chamber of Commerce survey, optimism versus pessimism)

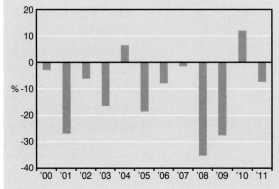

SourceL ONS

- Consumer confidence remains low leading to households delaying major purchases and thus holding down demand.

- Business confidence remains low (see Figure 7.11).

- Public sector contraction as part of the Coalition government austerity measures.

- Uncertainty surrounding the economic prospects in Eurozone economies such as Greece and Spain, with fears even of the break up (or at least reduction in the size of) the Eurozone itself.

- Slow recovery and political uncertainty (due to the presidential election of November 2012) in the USA.

- Signs of slowing growth in the main emerging market economies, or BRICs (Brazil, Russia, India, China).

One feature of the economic story of 2012 has been that of apparently declining productivity in the UK. Labour productivity is an important measure of the efficiency of an economy in converting labour into output (see Chapter 6).

In 2012, output per worker remained 3% lower than its peak before the recession. Reasons given by economists for this include:

*Figure 7.12: Output per worker*

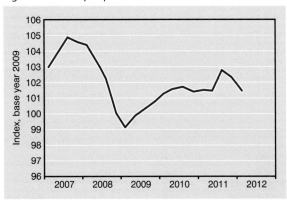

Source: ONS

*Figure 7.13: UK employment and unemployment (Labour Force Survey, change on previous month, 000s)*

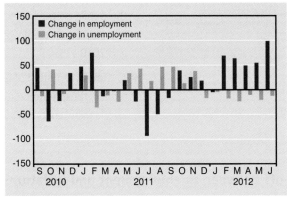

Source: HM Treasury

- 'Labour hoarding': businesses hold onto workers because they are expecting the economy to return to stronger growth imminently and they wish to avoid the costs associated with making redundancies and then re-hiring high quality workers. This can be a positive sign for the macroeconomy.

- Collapse in investment due to the banking crisis: if firms are finding cheap credit difficult to obtain, this will have hindered investment in capital which can boost labour productivity. This links to the third point, below:

- Falling real wages: a combination of a squeezed labour market and relatively high inflation has made hiring or retaining workers a more cost-effective solution than investing in more efficient technologies and capital.

- 'Zombie firms': this argument is that there are firms in the UK which remain in existence despite very low levels of output and investment. These firms are able to meet their debt repayments only because of very low interest rates, and they are not creating surplus profit required to fund investment programmes.

A further puzzle has been the *increase in employment*, even during a period where unemployment has been high.

Since February 2012 at least 50,000 jobs have been created in the UK labour market each month, considerably outweighing the increase in unemployment. Therefore rising unemployment *and* employment have to be seen in the context of a growing workforce.

Returning to the specific problems of youth and long-term unemployed, 2012 data shows that unemployment for recent school leavers (those aged 16-17) is as high as 37% for men and 36% for women (approximately 100,000 unemployment for each group). For the 18-24 age group, young men are more likely to be unemployed, with rates of 23% (506,000 men) and 16% (310,000 women). Over 1 million of the unemployed in the UK are therefore under the age of 25.

## ●● Application and Analysis: Unemployment and Recession

The recent periods of recession in 2008-09 and 2012 clearly illustrate the strong correlation between negative economic growth and increased unemployment. Figure 7.8 shows this relationship earlier in the chapter. In mid-2012, UK unemployment was approximately 2.5 million, of which roughly 1.5 million were men and 1 million were women. Factors accounting for this imbalance are:

- Continued job losses in the manufacturing sector due to industrialisation, which has traditionally employed a higher proportion of men than women.

● Lower participation rates of women in the workforce, particularly in the older age groups.

● Under the Labour government of recent years there was an increase in public sector employment which created more jobs, particularly for women.

The main solution to demand-deficient unemployment is to return the macroeconomy to strong growth. The prospect of such a recovery in the years ahead are discussed elsewhere in the book, but just as the pattern of unemployment is currently asymmetrical, it is likely that future trends in employment and unemployment will affect some groups and regions of the UK more favourably than others.

*Figure 7.14: Unemployment by region (% of workforce, September 2012)*

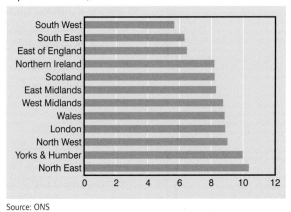

Source: ONS

Areas of key concern are:

● The impact of public sector employment reductions on regions outside London and the south-east; these are areas where the highest levels of public sector job creation occurred.

● The impact of public sector employment reductions on women; by some estimates, the proportion of female employment in the public sector increased at three times the rate of male employment between 2000 and 2010.

● The implementation of effective policies to reduce the phenomenon (and economic and social costs associated with) the 'NEETs' of the labour market.

## ● Analysis: **Is there a trade-off between unemployment and inflation?**

This section leads into the following chapter on inflation and deflation. Since the work of A W Phillips in the 1950s, there has been debate in economics around the exact relationship between two key macroeconomic variables: unemployment and inflation. The stable, negative correlation (**the Phillips curve**) was an important belief of the Keynesian school.

Table 7.1 shows data for unemployment and inflation data for the UK economy in recent years.

*Table 7.1: 'Phillips Curve' data: unemployment and inflation*

|  | LFS Unemployment (% of workforce) | Consumer Price Inflation (% p.a.) |  | LFS Unemployment (% of workforce) | Consumer Price Inflation (% p.a.) |
|---|---|---|---|---|---|
| 1993 | 10.4 | 2.5 | 2003 | 5.0 | 1.4 |
| 1994 | 9.5 | 2.0 | 2004 | 4.8 | 1.4 |
| 1995 | 8.6 | 2.6 | 2005 | 4.9 | 2.0 |
| 1996 | 8.1 | 2.5 | 2006 | 5.4 | 2.3 |
| 1997 | 6.9 | 1.8 | 2007 | 5.3 | 2.3 |
| 1998 | 6.2 | 1.6 | 2008 | 5.7 | 3.6 |
| 1999 | 6.0 | 1.4 | 2009 | 7.7 | 2.2 |
| 2000 | 5.4 | 0.8 | 2010 | 7.8 | 3.3 |
| 2001 | 5.1 | 1.2 | 2011 | 8.1 | 4.5 |
| 2002 | 5.2 | 1.3 |  |  |  |

Source: HM Treasury

## Question

2. Use the data from Table 7.1 to plot a Phillips curve with rate of unemployment on the horizontal axis and inflation on the vertical axis.

Economists have identified the **NAIRU** (the **n**on-**a**ccelerating **i**nflation **r**ate of **u**nemployment) as a useful point of reference. The theory suggests that any attempt to reduce unemployment below a certain level will lead to an increase in inflationary pressure. This is a similar concept to the Natural Rate of Unemployment, which suggests perhaps that there is an 'equilibrium' level of unemployment in the economy. Classical, or supply-side economists, argue that this unemployment persists not due to a lack of demand, but rather due to supply-side imperfections in the labour market such as excessive trade union power, minimum wage legislation, and an unwillingness on the part of the unemployed to actively search for work and take responsibility for their own joblessness.

Keynesian economists on the other hand stress the importance of demand-management policies such as fiscal and monetary expansion to increase aggregate demand (actual GDP) in the economy to create sufficient demand for labour and reduce unemployment.

The relationship between inflation and unemployment is actually a relationship of each variable to the central policy objective of economic growth. In times of strong GDP growth, unemployment tends to fall and inflationary pressure rises; in times of low or negative growth, unemployment rises and inflationary pressure recedes.

*Figure 7.15: UK and EU unemployment (% of workforce, ILO measure)*

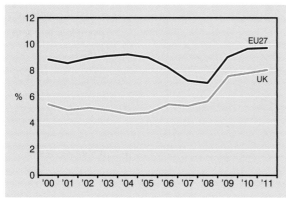

Source: HM Treasury

*Figure 7.16: UK and selected other EU members unemployment rates (% of workforce, ILO measure)*

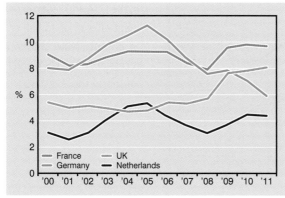

Source: HM Treasury/OECD and Eurostat

The data in Table 7.1 does not show a clear linear relationship because not all unemployment is caused by a lack of growth (structural and frictional factors also exist) and not all inflation is caused by excessive demand (cost-push pressures can also increase prices, as experienced in the recent recession where CPI remained stubbornly above its upper target of 3% until 2012).

● Application: **An international comparison of unemployment**

Figure 7.15 shows how UK unemployment, even during the recent recession, has remained below the average for the 27 members of the European Union.

The story within the EU, however, is far more complex than the average data suggests.

Until the 2008-09 recession, unemployment in most EU economies was stable, if not uniform across the EU. However, some economies were hit particularly hard and the unemployment data for Portugal, Italy, Ireland, Greece and Spain (the 'PIIGS' of Europe) is shown in Figure 7.17.

*Which of the PIIGS has experienced the most dramatic increase in unemployment since 2005?*

*Figure 7.17: PIIGS unemployment (% of workforce, ILO measure)*

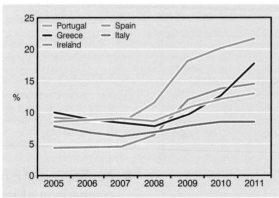

Source: HM Treasury/OECD and Eurostat

## Questions

3. How stable is the relationship that you have drawn between the level of unemployment and the rate of price inflation?

4. Which of the PIIGS has experienced the most dramatic increase in unemployment since 2005? And which has the strongest unemployment record of those shown?

*Figure 7.18: EU27 unemployment compared to Japan and the USA (% of workforce, ILO measure)*

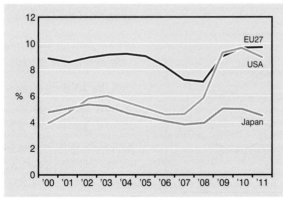

Source: HM Treasury/OECD and Eurostat

Globally, the EU27 average is compared to other major economies in Figure 7.18.

Throughout the early 2000s, unemployment in the USA and Japan experienced unemployment rates of up to half of those experienced in Europe. Note the impact of the recent recession in the USA, and the relatively minor impact of this 'Western' crisis on Japan.

# Chapter 8

# Inflation and Deflation

This chapter looks at the difference between the Retail Price Index and the Consumer Price Index, as well as how they portray trends in price changes over the last decade differently. It goes on to look at recent price changes in various sectors before comparing UK inflation with that of other countries. An examination of the fluctuations in the rate of inflation over the last 10 years follows before a final discussion on the dangers of deflation.

## ●● Knowledge and Application: Defining and measuring UK inflation

Inflation is defined as a sustained increase in the general price level.

A key point to note here is that the price of some goods and services might be falling, but the *average* price of goods and services in the economy is rising. As prices rise, the value of a given amount of money falls as it can purchase fewer goods and services.

There are two main measures of inflation in the UK:

### 1. Consumer Price Index (CPI)

The CPI index has been used to measure the official rate of inflation in the UK since December 2003 (previously it was the Retail Price Index which is the second measure discussed below). The Bank of England targets inflation at 2.0% according to the CPI measure (see Chapter 9). This measure uses the same methodology as the *Harmonised Index of Consumer Prices* (*HICP*) measure, which is used by economies across the EU. The ECB uses this measure to assess rates of inflation in the Eurozone. The Labour government switched to the CPI measure so that UK inflation could be compared directly with economies in the EU.

The CPI is a weighted index measuring the average price increase of a basket goods and services purchased by a typical household. The Office for National Statistics' (ONS) Expenditure and Food Survey measures the price changes of 700 goods and services purchased from an average household. Each item is weighted according to the proportion of household income that is spent on it. Therefore, if twice as much income is spent by households on clothes than on video games, then clothing should receive twice the weighting.

To ensure that the CPI measure accurately reflects changes in the cost of living, amendments are made annually to the items that are included in the basket so that changes in consumer habits are reflected. In 2012 tablet computers were included for the first time, while processed film was excluded.

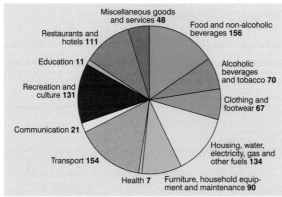

*Figure 8.1: CPI group weightings 1996*

Source: ONS   Total = 1000

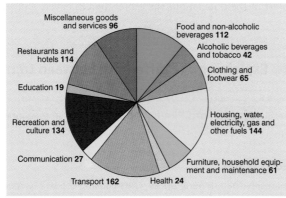

*Figure 8.2: CPI group weightings 2012*

Source: ONS   Total = 1000

Similarly, changes are made to the weightings that items receive each year. In 2012 gas bills were given a higher weighting, due to significant rises in gas prices over the previous year causing households to spend a larger proportion of their income on gas.

### 2. Retail Price Index (RPI)

The RPI was the official measure of inflation from 1947 until 2003. The RPI is measured in a very similar way to the CPI, but also includes some items omitted in the CPI, such as council tax, mortgage interest payments and buildings insurance. As a result, many believe that the inclusion of vital housing costs makes the RPI a better measure of changes in the average cost of living of UK households. The RPI is still used by the government for various purposes such as to set rent increases in social housing, and to calculate amounts payable on index linked gilts. Furthermore, employers often use the RPI as a basis for discussions on wage increases.

### Questions

1. Calculate the percentage change in the proportion of household expenditure on (i) clothing and footwear, and (ii) transport, between 1996 and 2012.

2. Explain the possible causes of a decrease in the share of household spending on food and non-alcoholic beverages.

3. Explain the possible causes of an increase in the share of spending on transport.

### ● Knowledge: **Explaining differences between the RPI and CPI**

There are some important distinctions in the way these two indices are measured:

1. There is an important statistical difference in how the RPI and CPI measures are calculated; the CPI uses a geometric mean, while the RPI uses an arithmetic mean.

2. The CPI excludes some vital housing costs that are included in the RPI, namely Council tax, mortgage interest payments, house depreciation, buildings insurance, ground rent, solar electricity (PV) Feed-In Tariffs and other house purchase costs such as estate agents' and conveyance fees.

3. The RPI index excludes some items included in the CPI measure, such as university tuition fees and stockbroker fees.

4. The weightings given in the CPI index are based on the spending patterns of all households in the UK, tourists visiting the UK, and those living in institutional accommodation such as university halls of residence. CPI weightings are based on household spending in the National Accounts. On the contrary, the RPI weightings are based on the Expenditure and Food Survey. Furthermore, the RPI excludes the top 4% of households in the income distribution and pensioners, as their consumption patterns are significantly different to the rest of the population. Therefore, the CPI covers a broader section of the population.

### ●● Application and Analysis: **Explaining the difference between trends in the CPI and RPI**

Figure 8.3 shows that since the introduction of CPI inflation as the official measure in 2003, RPI has generally been higher. This is due to:

### 1. The inclusion of housing costs in RPI

Housing costs tend to rise more quickly than general prices, thus causing the RPI to measure a higher rate of inflation. In 2009 however, the RPI plummeted, showing a brief period of negative inflation. This was

Figure 8.3: UK CPI and RPI inflation
(Jan 2003 – Aug 2012)

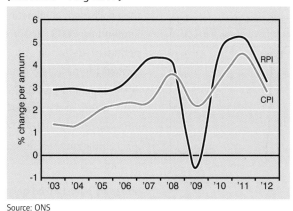

Source: ONS

due to dramatic cuts in interest rates, from 5.0% in April 2008 to 0.5% in March 2009, which reduced mortgage interest payments considerably.

**2. The different 'mean' calculations**

An arithmetic mean ($\Sigma x/n$), used in calculating the RPI, tends to give a higher figure than a geometric mean ($((X1)(X2)\ldots (Xn))^{1/n}$), which is used in the CPI. According to the ONS, the different calculation of the 'mean' is the most important reason inflation on the RPI measure tends to be higher than that calculated by the CPI.

● **Evaluation: Problems with using RPI or CPI indices**

There are several problems with using the RPI or CPI as accurate measures of inflation. They are:

1. The CPI and RPI both measure the *average* rate of inflation, faced by a *typical* household. In reality, individuals and households have very different consumption baskets, and thus have varied rates of inflation.

2. Both measures do not take into account changes in the quality of goods and services, and thus might overstate inflation. If you bought a car today you would get a lot more for your money compared to a car purchased in 1970 e.g. electric windows, central locking, airbags, a GPS navigation system etc.

3. After CPI was adopted as the official measure of inflation in 2003, many public and private sector employers started to use CPI inflation as a basis for wage negotiation rather than RPI, indexing wage increases to the CPI rate. When the two indices were close together in 2004-5 this was not much of a problem, but in 2006-7 when RPI outpaced CPI the policy to use CPI became controversial, as many felt they were receiving real pay cuts. However, when RPI fell well below CPI in 2008-9, those same employees were arguably receiving pay rises in real terms. Whether the CPI or RPI best reflect the cost of living increases faced by employees depends on a number of factors, but home ownership is undoubtedly very important. For those with mortgages the RPI is likely to be a more accurate measure, as mortgage interest payments are included. This highlights a key problem; it is very difficult to find a measure that accurately reflects cost of living changes for whole groups of employees.

● ● Application and Analysis: **Recent trends in UK inflation**

Inflation according to the RPI measure peaked at 9.5% in 1990 at the end of the so-called 'Lawson boom'. Between 1992 and 2004 inflation was very stable according to all measures. Shortly after being given their independence the Bank of England wanted to show that they were tough on inflation, and raised the base rate of interest from 5.9375% in April to 7.25% in November of that year, quelling fears that strong growth at that time would lead to rising inflation. This rate rise, combined with other factors (explained later) caused inflationary pressures to subside. Between 1997 and 2003 the base rate of interest was historically very stable, and fell during this period reaching 3.5% in July 2003, as seen in Figure 8.4. Between late 2003 and mid 2007 inflationary pressures grew and both CPI and RPI increased, as shown in Figure 8.3. To counter this, the Bank of England raised the base rate of interest incrementally from 3.5% in November 2003 to 5.75% in July 2007. After overshooting the 'acceptable limit' of 3% in March 2007 (3.1%), CPI inflation fell below target to 1.8% by September of that year. From then, however, inflation rose

Figure 8.4: Bank of England base rate 1999-2012, with forecasts to 2015

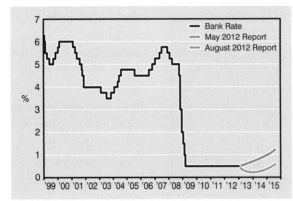

Source: Bank of England, August 2012, *Inflation Report*

Figure 8.5: CPI in goods and services 1997-2011

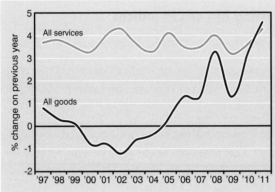

Source: ONS

Figure 8.6: Changes in consumer prices in selected categories of goods and services

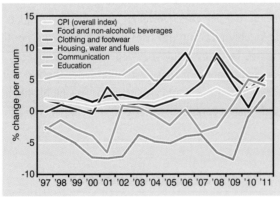

Source: ONS

considerably, reaching 5.2% according to the CPI measure by September 2008. Inflation then collapsed, plummeting to 1.1% (CPI) by September 2009. To prevent a sustained period of deflation, the Bank of England slashed the base rate during 2008 and early 2009, reaching just 0.5% by March of that year, where it has remained, despite CPI inflation climbing to 5.2% by September 2011. Inflation then subsided, reaching 2.4% by June 2012.

So far we have looked only at overall inflation for goods and services. However, once we disaggregate the data, we can reveal a number of trends which are hidden by aggregate inflation figures:

1. Figure 8.5 shows that for most of the period 1997 to 2011, goods inflation was considerably lower than services inflation. In fact, according to the CPI measure, the average price of goods was falling between 2000 and 2004. Services, by contrast, saw steady price increases of around 3.5-4.0% per annum throughout the period. This means that the cause of low inflation between 1997 and 2004 was due to minimal price rises of goods, while inflation in services was present throughout this period.

2. Since 2005 goods inflation has been on an upward trajectory. Despite falls in goods inflation from 2006 to 2007, and from 2008 to 2009, goods inflation increased quite dramatically, rising above that of the rate of services inflation by 2011. Therefore, it was abnormally high inflation in goods, rather than services, that caused overall CPI inflation to break 5% in the autumns of 2009 and 2011.

3. Figure 8.6 shows the very different rates of inflation in different sectors between 1997 and 2011. Price rises in education were high throughout the period due to large private school fee increases, and the introduction of variable top-up fees for degree courses for the academic year 2006-7. Increases in housing, water and fuel costs were much higher during the second half of the period than the first, as was the case for food. The inflation for clothing and footwear, which had been negative for much of the period, became positive in 2011 underlining the trend of rising goods inflation towards the end of the period.

## ● Application: **International comparison of inflation rates**

During the 1970s and much of the 1980s the UK was known as 'the sick man of Europe', in part owing to her poor inflation record. Since the early 1990s the UK's inflation record has been much improved. Figure 8.7 shows that the average rate of inflation in the UK from 2001 to 2011 has been similar to that of many of her competitors, and below the OECD average. However, this data hides trends which have taken place within this time period. Figure 8.8 shows that during 2001-2005, the UK enjoyed lower inflation rates than most of her competitors. From 2005 onwards, the UK performs poorly relative to her competitors, with inflation rates higher than the G7 and EU27 averages.

*Figure 8.7: Average annual percentage change in CPI, 2001-2011*

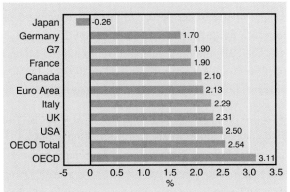

Source: OECD

*Figure 8.8: Inflation rates (CPI annual % change) for selected countries 2001-2011*

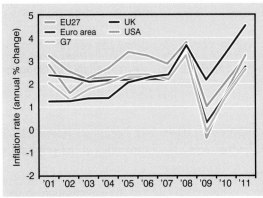
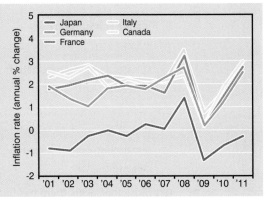

Source: HM Treasury

### Question

4. Explain why inflation rates in the UK exceeded those of her main competitors between 2006 and 2011.

## ● Analysis: **Explanations for low UK inflation 1992-2004**

There are several explanations for low inflation in the UK in the final decade of the last century. They are:

### 1. The strong pound

During this period the value of pound rose significantly, and was at a level considerably higher than during the early to mid 1990s (look back at Figure 5.14). This put downward pressure on the price of imports, meaning that overall price increases of goods in particular, were restrained. A stronger pound reduces the price of services and finished goods, but also lowers the price of raw materials used to make products in the UK. The UK is a relatively open economy with the value of imports exceeding 30% of GDP. Therefore, lower import prices due to a strong pound had a significant effect.

### 2. A lack of exogenous shocks

During the 1970s there were a number of hikes in the price of essential sources of energy. The price of oil rose from under $5 per barrel in 1970 to over $25 by 1980. This was a major contributing factor to a period

of stagflation (high unemployment and high inflation) in the UK at that time. The period 1992-2004 however, saw no major exogenous shocks, and commodity prices remained reasonably stable which kept cost-push inflationary pressures in check.

### 3. Competitive product markets

(i) Domestic factors: The 1980s and 1990s saw a period of privatisation and deregulation. This led to greater competition, especially in the utility sector, which put downward pressure on prices. Furthermore, a tougher approach by government towards competition policy was adopted. The Competition Act of 1998 saw the Competition Commission replacing the Monopolies and Mergers Commission, and the 2002 Enterprise Act gave the new Commission far more power than its predecessor. The effect was to encourage competition across many sectors.

(ii) Global factors: During this period many countries joined the WTO and the global economy more generally. The UK faced rising competition from newly-industrialised countries (NICs) such as from China, India and countries in Eastern Europe. These countries have much lower unit labour costs, and thus have a comparative advantage in labour-intensive industries. As a result, UK manufacturers faced stiff competition from overseas and were forced to reduce mark-ups and costs. This effect, along with greater import volume of goods from NICs, put downward pressure on the price of basic manufactures such as clothing, footwear, and household items, as shown in Figure 8.6.

### 4. Flexible labour markets

Three factors made the UK's Labour market more flexible during this period:

(i) Greater female participation in the workforce increased the supply of labour and reduced wage-inflationary pressures.

(ii) Significant immigration from outside and inside the EU increased the supply of labour and helped to plug skills shortages in certain industries. On 1st January 2004 ten new countries, mostly from Central and Eastern Europe joined the EU. Afterwards a significant influx of self-selecting, productive workers came to the UK.

(iii) Since the 1980s there has been a significant amount of 'de-unionisation' in the UK, partly due to government policy in the 1980s, and partly due to the relative decline of the more unionised manufacturing sector. Wage bargaining power has declined as a result, reducing cost-push inflationary pressures.

### 5. Credible monetary policy

After gaining independence in 1997 the Bank of England acted quickly when there were signs of growing inflationary pressure by raising interest rates. Such pre-emptive action and a clearly defined policy framework helped to build faith in the Bank of England's ability to keep inflation within the 1-3% acceptable boundary. This helped to lower *inflationary expectations*, and thus wage demands remained subdued during this period.

## ● Analysis: Explanations for the higher rates of inflation 2008-2012

From 2008-12 inflation has been more volatile than in the previous 15 years, but the trend has undoubtedly been for higher inflation during this period. There are several reasons for this:

### 1. Higher commodity prices

Since 2007 there has been a significant increase in the price of many commodities, most importantly for the UK economy oil and food have risen in price substantially.

As shown in Figure 8.9 the price of oil rose from $30 per barrel at the start of 2004 to over $130 per barrel in mid-2008. The oil price then collapsed with the onset of the global recession in 2009 but recovered

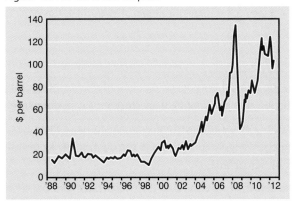

Figure 8.9: Brent crude oil price

Source: Oilnergy.com

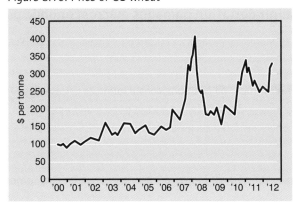

Figure 8.10: Price of US wheat

Source: Food and Agriculture Organisation of the UN

strongly. In 2012 the oil price remained historically very high despite real fears of a second global recession. The sustained high oil price is due to growing demand from developing economies, and slow production growth due to dwindling stocks. Higher oil prices push up the cost of production of many goods and services, thus contributing to higher cost-push inflationary pressures.

Food prices started to rise rapidly after 2006, owing to more wheat being used for bio-fuels rather than food production, increased global demand due to world population growth, and rising demand for meat by consumers in NICs. Although food prices fell back during the global recession of 2008-9 they have since risen, as Figure 8.10 shows is reflected in the upward trend in the price of US wheat, and in 2012 there were fears of an imminent food crisis after a drought in the mid-West of the United States caused food prices to rise sharply.

### 2. A weaker pound

Since the peak in the trade-weighted value of sterling in early 2007 the pound depreciated considerably, losing almost 30% of its value by early 2009, as was shown in Figure 5.14. Despite gains against the euro since then, the pound remains considerably weaker than during 'the NICE decade'. This causes the price of imports to rise, raising the overall price level.

### 3. Inflation and wage inflation in newly-industrialising countries (NICs)

Since the mid-2000s a number of NICs, including India and China, have been suffering from high inflation, and high wage inflation. In China for example, the wage gap to advanced economies has shrunk rapidly in recent years, in part due to hikes in the minimum wage. This has caused the price of cheap manufactured imports to rise, and overall goods inflation has increased as a result, as shown in Figure 8.5.

### 4. VAT increases

The rate of Value Added Tax (VAT), which is paid on most goods and services in the UK was cut from 17.5% to 15% on 1st December 2008 to try to stimulate consumption as the economy fell into a deep recession. The rate of VAT returned to 17.5% in January 2010, and was then raised to 20% on 4th January 2011 by the new Chancellor George Osborne, as part of the government's fiscal deficit reduction strategy. Both of these VAT increases had a significant impact in pushing up the price of goods and services.

## Extension material: 'Core' inflation

A measure of 'core' inflation can be useful as it excludes price changes in volatile items such as food and energy. Therefore, it is a reasonable measure of 'underlying' inflationary pressure in the economy. However, as high commodity prices seem to be a more permanent feature than during 'the NICE decade', cost-push,

rather than demand-pull pressures could be the main cause of inflation for several years to come. 'Core' inflation therefore, might not be a very good predictor of actual changes in the rate of inflation.

## ● Knowledge: **Deflation**

Deflation is a sustained **fall** in the general price level. It is important to distinguish between deflation which may be harmful, and deflation that does not harm macroeconomic performance.

(i)  Deflation may occur due to technological advances and productivity gains that cause long-run economic growth. As the long-run aggregate supply curve shifts to the right, there is downward pressure on the price level. This is known as *benign deflation*.

(ii)  However, a lack of aggregate demand may also cause the overall price level to fall. This has been a persistent problem in Japan since the 1990s, as shown in Figure 8.8. This type is known as *malign deflation*.

## ● Analysis: **Reasons why malign deflation damages macroeconomic performance**

There are several reasons why deflation due to a lack of aggregate demand is a problem:

### 1. Deferred consumption
If consumers see prices falling today, they will postpone consumption as prices will be lower in the future. Therefore, consumption and aggregate demand fall, reducing growth and employment. The resulting fall in the price level further entrenches the deflation problem.

### 2. Rising real value of debt
As prices fall, nominal wages may fall as well. Employers may try to justify cuts in nominal wages when prices are falling. In addition, as aggregate demand in the economy is weak, workers are in a weak bargaining position. As nominal wages fall, it becomes harder for households to repay their debts, as their nominal value remains unchanged. This means that households must allocate a greater proportion of income towards debt repayment, and cut back on consumption.

### 3. Monetary policy becomes ineffective
Deflation can cause monetary policy to become a significantly less powerful policy instrument. To try to boost aggregate demand and prevent a persistent period of deflation from occurring, a central bank will cut interest rates. However, if interest rates are cut by 1%, but prices fall by 2%, the **real interest rate** has actually risen, which encourages saving and discourages consumer spending. Moreover, once interest rates have been cut to zero, there is nothing more that interest changes can do to inflate aggregate demand, thus rendering monetary policy ineffective.

### 4. Large fiscal deficits and debt burdens emerge
As monetary policy becomes ineffective in stimulating aggregate demand, the government must adopt an expansionary fiscal policy instead. A sustained budget deficit could lead to excessive levels of national debt being accumulated, which will create a drag on growth in the long term. This is what happened in Japan, where national debt reached 211% of GDP by 2012.

## Essay Questions

5. Examine the effects of a rise in the price of oil upon UK macroeconomic performance.

6. Evaluate the view that adjusting interest rates is the best way to manage the rate of inflation in the UK.

7. 'Deflation is always bad for macroeconomic performance'. To what extent do you agree with this statement?

# Chapter 9

# Monetary Policy in the UK

Monetary policy is defined as government policy regarding interest rates, exchange rates and the money supply. Since 1992 the UK has had a floating exchange rate, and thus the value of the pound is not deliberately altered by policy makers. Until recently monetary policy in effect meant the setting of interest rates, but in 2009 the Bank of England started to use a new policy; **quantitative easing**. The Monetary Policy Committee at the Bank of England are the focal point of this chapter; the committee members themselves, the tools they use to target inflation, and how successful they have been in achieving their objective.

## ● ● Knowledge **and** Application: **The UK monetary policy framework**

On 6th May 1997 the newly-elected government announced plans to give the Bank of England independence, which was achieved under the 1998 Bank of England Act. The Monetary Policy Committee (MPC) at the Bank of England was given operational independence for setting interest rates to achieve **price stability**, while supporting the government's targets for growth and employment. Those in favour of independence argued that by being free of political interference, the Bank of England should gain credibility for controlling inflation. The MPC contains 9 members.

The MPC's task is to achieve the inflation target by adjusting the base rate. The base rate (also known as the repo rate) is the interest rate at which the Bank of England lends to commercial banks. Since 2003 the Bank of England has had an inflation target of 2.0% on the CPI measure, with a symmetrical 'acceptable boundary' of between 1% and 3%.

It takes up to two years for the full effect for a change in the interest rate to have its impact upon aggregate demand and therefore inflation. As a result, the MPC makes interest rate decisions to try to achieve the inflation target in two years time, and therefore acts in a *pre-emptive* manner, rather than in response to recent changes in the inflation rate. The MPC gathers information to predict inflation into the future, and adjust the base rate to try to bring future inflation back to target. One good example of the pre-emptive setting of the interest rate came in late 2008. As outlined in Chapter 1 the Bank of England cut the base rate from 4.5% to 0.5% between October 2008 and March 2009 despite the fact that inflation remained above target throughout this period (see Figure 1.6). In fact, when the base rate was cut on 4th October 2008 the previous month's CPI inflation rate was 5.2%, the highest level since 1992. The MPC was cutting rates as they predicted a fall in core inflationary pressure as the economy fell into recession.

The MPC meets for two and a half days each month. They usually meet on the first Wednesday and Thursday of each month with a half day 'pre-meeting' on the Friday before. On the Wednesday members receive a wealth of data on the domestic and global economy from Bank of England economists and regional representatives. The data includes developments in trade, investment, financial markets, productivity, the budget balance and many other indicators. Ultimately the Bank is trying to decide how strong domestic demand will be relative to the productive capacity of the economy, in effect, predicting the future output gap. If domestic demand is growing faster than the economy's productive potential then inflationary pressure will be forecast to grow, and interest rates should be raised.

On the basis of the data the MPC members must decide if inflation is set to hit the target in two years time. Members then vote on whether to hold, raise, or cut the base rate. Each member has one vote, and the majority decision is implemented. Recent disagreements on the MPC came in early 2011, when Andrew Sentance voted for a half point rise in the base rate between February and his departure from the MPC in May. Most members considered the rise in commodity prices that was causing inflation at the time to be a 'one-off shock', and that core-inflationary pressure was low, thus there was no need to raise the base rate.

Andrew Sentance argued that rising commodity prices were more of a permanent feature in the global economy, and an appreciation of the exchange rate resulting from a base rate increase would lower inflationary pressure and stop higher expectations of inflation becoming built into wage-bargaining, which would choke off the recovery at that time.

## Questions

1. The Monetary Policy Committee (MPC) is most likely to raise interest rates if:
   A. Unemployment is rising.
   B. The exchange rate is appreciating.
   C. The growth of the money supply is decreasing.
   D. Domestic demand is set to rise above the level of potential GDP.

2. Explain the difficulty in measuring the size of an output gap.

Due to the important role of expectations, monetary policy is most likely to be successful if the Bank of England have *credibility*. That is, the public believe in the MPC's ability to control inflation. A number of measures have been used to try to achieve this:

(i) The workings of the MPC are transparent, and members are accountable. The minutes of the meeting are published two weeks after the meeting, and show how each member voted. Those in the minority are asked to state the action they would have preferred.

(ii) Members of the MPC regularly appear before parliamentary committees, usually the Treasury Select Committee, to answer questions about their decisions. The MPC is also accountable to the Court of the Bank, comprising of experts in commerce, industry and finance.

(iii) If the rate of inflation goes outside of the 1-3% 'acceptable' limits the Governor of the Bank of England must write an Open Letter to the Chancellor of the Exchequer to explain why the inflation target has been missed, and how he/she intends to rectify this.

(iv) The *Inflation Report*, published each quarter, provides details on recent developments in the economy and monetary policy, justifying the MPC's actions.

(v) Perhaps most importantly, the MPC is made up of experts from a wide variety of backgrounds including academics, monetary policy experts and economists from industry.

The 9 members of the Monetary Policy Committee as in December 2012

| | |
|---|---|
| Mervyn King | Governor of the Bank of England |
| Charles Bean | Deputy Governor (responsible for monetary policy) |
| Paul Tucker | Deputy Governor (responsible for financial stability) |
| Spencer Dale | Executive Director for Monetary Analysis and Statistics |
| Paul Fisher | Executive Director for Markets |
| David Miles | External member, former Chief UK Economist of Morgan Stanley |
| Ian McCafferty | External member, former Chief Economic Adviser to the CBI |
| Martin Weale | External member, former Director of NIESR |
| Ben Broadbent | External member, Chief European Economist at Goldman Sachs |

## ● Analysis: **Why does the UK have an inflation target?**

There are several advantages from having a specific 2.0% inflation target:

1. Reducing inflationary expectations
   By having a *credible* 2.0% target, workers will moderate their wage claims accordingly, as they can achieve real income growth without large pay demands. This reduces cost-push inflationary pressures. Similarly, businesses will avoid large price increases if prices across the economy are not expected to rise significantly.

2. Failure of targeting 'intermediate variables'

   *Intermediate* variables (i.e. variables which influence the rate of inflation such as the exchange rate or the money supply) can be targeted rather than inflation itself. During the 1980s there was no specific inflation target. Instead, the Thatcher government tried to control the money supply but it continued to grow. Targeting inflation directly allows policy-makers to consider all the factors that influence inflation, rather than fixating on one or two.

3. Keeping *fiat* money credible

   The value of money is no longer tied to gold. Instead, *fiat* money is only worth something because people believe it has value, and one of the most important jobs of any government is to preserve the value of money. Therefore, it is beneficial to have a monetary policy framework which protects against inflation and helps people to believe that their money will have almost the same worth tomorrow as today.

4. Success of inflation targeting elsewhere

   Inflation targeting has proved effective in other countries, particularly in New Zealand and Canada after they adopted the policy in the early 1990s.

## ● Analysis: **The transmission mechanism of monetary policy**

Changes in interest rates affect inflation primarily through their impact on aggregate demand, and also through changes in the price of imported goods and services. A fall in interest rates, such as the fall in the base rate from 5.0% to 0.5% between April 2008 and March 2009 could impact upon the economy via a number of channels:

1. Household saving and borrowing

   Lower interest rates reduce the cost of borrowing, and reduce the return on saving. This should raise the level of borrowing and reduce the savings ratio, thus increasing consumption and aggregate demand. Demand for consumer durables (e.g. cars, computers) should rise significantly, as they are usually purchased on credit.

2. Mortgage repayments and effective disposable income

   According to the Financial Services Authority (FSA) around 70% of mortgages in the UK are variable rate mortgages. Therefore, a fall in the interest rate will mean that monthly mortgage repayments will fall, increasing the effective disposable income of homeowners. This should boost consumption and hence aggregate demand. This effect is especially significant for the UK, as around 67% of households were 'owner-occupied' in 2012, far higher than most of Europe.

3. Asset prices and the 'wealth effect'

   As interest rates fall, the return on holding cash savings accounts diminishes. Therefore savers and investors in search of a better return are more likely to purchase equities or property, thus increasing their demand and value. Furthermore, more people will be tempted to buy property when interest rates are low, as mortgage payments will be lower. This puts further upward pressure on property prices. As asset prices rise, people see their wealth value increase and 'feel' richer, boosting consumer confidence and consumption. In addition, some households will take out loans against the rising value of their properties, adding to consumption. This is known as 'equity withdrawal'.

4. Investment and the 'hurdle rate'

   At any point in time firms have a number of potential investment projects. The hurdle rate is the minimum expected return a company demands before it goes ahead with a project given the risks involved. Many investments are funded through borrowing. As interest rates fall, the expected return of a project rises as the cost of the project has fallen. Therefore more projects become profitable, so more will go ahead, thus increasing overall investment and aggregate demand.

5. The exchange rate, net exports and import prices

As interest rates fall, there is a **hot money** outflow as international investors see a fall on their return from keeping money in UK banks. This causes demand for the pound to fall, resulting in a currency depreciation. As a result, exports become more attractive while imports become more expensive, resulting in a rise in net exports. Furthermore, a rise in the price of imports directly raises the price level.

*Figure 9.1: The monetary policy transmission mechanism*

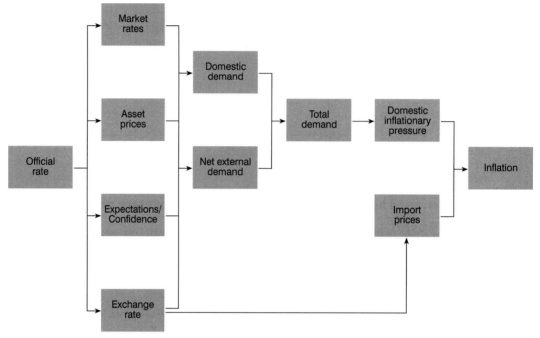

Source: Bank of England

## ● Evaluation: **The effects of a fall in interest rates**

Making accurate forecasts over the impact of a fall in interest rates is difficult for several reasons:

1. Time lags – Commercial banks do not immediately adjust their retail rates in response to a fall in the base rate, and it takes a further year for the full impact of a change in aggregate demand to affect inflation.

2. Asymmetric impact on households – Individuals who rely heavily on savings (e.g. pensioners) will see their income from interest fall in response to a fall in the base rate, and thus their spending may fall. However, this effect is outweighed by higher borrowing, less saving and more spending from most households, raising aggregate demand overall.

3. Asymmetric impact on firms – Some firms will see their income from cash deposits fall, potentially reducing their level of investment. However, across all firms, lower interest rates tend to boost investment levels due to the lower cost of borrowing to finance investment projects.

4. Some mortgages are fixed rate – Some mortgages in the UK offer fixed rates of interest, and thus monthly repayments will not fall in response to a base rate cut until the term of the fixed rate expires, and the terms of the mortgage are renegotiated. However, most mortgages in the UK are 'variable rate'.

5. De-coupling – When the Bank of England cut the base rate dramatically between late 2008 and early 2009, rates on key personal loans such as credit cards and overdrafts actually increased as is shown in Figure 9.2. This was due to banks trying to repair their balance sheets in the wake of the financial crisis, higher interbank lending rates and the banks attaching a higher 'risk premium' to lending during a time of recession and enormous uncertainty.

*Figure 9.2: Bank Rate and quoted interest rates on new household borrowing*

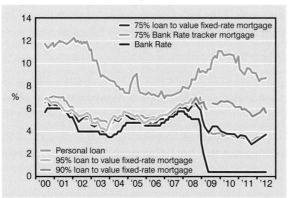

Source: Bank of England

6. Willingness to borrow/lend – Despite the significant base rate cuts between late 2008 and early 2009, the savings rate rose considerably due to falling consumer confidence, and households became less willing to borrow as consumers prepared for a 'rainy day'. Simultaneously, banks became less willing to lend, which harmed SMEs who struggled to access much needed credit.

## ● Evaluation: How well has the UK monetary policy framework worked?

Since the Bank of England was granted control of the base rate of interest with the objective of controlling inflation in 1997 most would argue that the effect has been broadly positive, especially in the first 10 years. There are several reasons for this:

● From Bank of England independence in May 1997 right through to March 2007 inflation stayed within the target range.

● The MPC was praised by the House of Commons Treasury Select Committee for establishing a credible inflation targeting record.

● The UK's inflation performance was stronger than most of her European and North American competitors between 1997 and 2007.

● The Bank of England were effective in pre-empting future inflationary pressure and taking action as demonstrated by repeated rate rises in early 2004, when the MPC lifted the bank rate by a full percentage point which caused inflation to fall back to target by the end of 2005.

● In 1997 Mervyn King acknowledged the Bank of England's role in supporting other macroeconomic objectives, particularly growth and employment. He stated that central bankers should not be 'inflation nutters' i.e. they should not focus purely on controlling inflation at the expense of growth and employment, a popular criticism of the European Central Bank (ECB). The MPC's significant base rate cuts in 2001 were effective in preventing a major downturn.

However, there has also been some criticism of the MPC and the extent of critical views has grown since 2007:

● The UK's inflation performance has worsened considerably since the beginning of the financial crisis in the autumn of 2007, both relative to the UK's main competitors and in relation to the inflation target. Between September 2007 and September 2012 CPI inflation was above the 3% upper acceptable boundary for 40 out of 60 months. During this time Mervyn King has had to write 14 Open Letters to the Chancellor explaining why the MPC have failed to keep inflation within the 1-3% boundary, whereas no letters were written during the previous 10 years.

● Some argue that the MPC has not always reacted quickly enough to changes in inflationary pressure. Inflationary pressure started to rise from the beginning of 2006 but the MPC did not raise the base rate until August of that year. More significant however, was the MPC's late reaction in cutting interest rates as the UK economy fell into a deep recession in 2008. GDP had been falling since the second quarter of 2008, but inflation reached 5.2% in September of that year largely due to a temporary commodity price

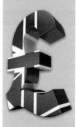

spike. Critics argue that the MPC should have recognised that these pressures were temporary, and that underlying inflationary pressure at the time was falling dramatically due to collapsing demand and rising unemployment. The Bank of England cut the base rate aggressively from 5.0% in October 2008 to 0.5% in March 2009, but this was not enough to stop CPI inflation falling well below target, and the RPI measure indicating a significant period of deflation for much of 2009.

● Some believe that the MPC's objectives have become blurred in recent years, thus eroding their credibility for inflation targeting. Critics argue that since the 2008-9 recession more emphasis has been put on growth rather than targeting inflation. During 2010 inflationary pressure grew significantly, and CPI inflation averaged 4.5% in 2011. Yet the Bank of England did not raise interest rates, keeping the base rate at the historic low of 0.5%. The fact that the UK economy fell back into recession during the final quarter of 2011 suggests that the Bank of England sided with supporting growth rather than controlling inflation. Supporters of the MPC are quick to point out that much of this inflation was due to temporary factors beyond their control (such as the VAT rise to 20% and energy price increases) and that underlying pressures remained weak. Inflation did fall back to below 3% by May 2012.

● Critics have argued that monetary policy has been operating under a 'one tool, one target' framework which has focussed too much on targeting overall price increases while ignoring the impact of policy instruments on key asset prices such as house prices. Although monetary policy was effective in controlling overall price increases during 'the NICE decade' (1997-2007), double digit house price inflation was the norm. In the UK and the US an extended period of low interest rates and high credit availability, especially in the early 2000s, fuelled a house price bubble which may have boosted consumer confidence and prevented deflation in the short term, but increased the risk of deflation when the bubble burst in 2007-8. There has been much debate amongst economists since the financial crisis on whether central banks should try to control credit growth and asset prices to try to prevent future bubbles emerging. The Bank of England is also considering strengthening the resilience of the banking system during credit booms. Whatever the outcome, asset prices will at least be monitored and given more attention in the future.

## Quantitative easing

By March 2009 the base rate had been cut to a historic low of 0.5% in an attempt to boost aggregate demand, but the UK economy remained in a deep recession and there was a continued threat of deflation. As a result, the MPC decided to try something new called **Quantitative Easing (QE)**.

By late 2012 £375bn had been created electronically by the Bank of England and placed into an 'Asset Purchase Facility'. This money is then used to buy illiquid assets, mostly government bonds, from financial institutions in exchange for more liquid cash. As a result, financial institutions have more loanable funds which can be passed onto households and firms, thus boosting aggregate demand, and putting upward pressure on prices. As the Bank of England is a big buyer in the bonds ('gilts') market, higher demand for bonds increases their price, reducing the yields and interest rates on bonds, which are the benchmark for some mortgage rates, bank overdraft rates and business borrowing rates. This should encourage spending and borrowing. Crucially, the Bank of England uses the newly-created money to purchase gilts from private investors such as pension funds and insurance companies. These investors typically do not want to hold on to this money, because it yields a low return. So they tend to use it to purchase other assets, such as corporate bonds and shares. That lowers longer-term borrowing costs and encourages the issuance of new equities and bonds which should increase asset prices, confidence and overall spending in the economy.

### Arguments in favour of quantitative easing
1. The supply of credit should increase due to greater liquidity in the financial system, as should the demand for credit due to lower interest rates. This should boost aggregate demand and put upward pressure on prices.

2. The Bank of England base rate cannot be lowered much further, thus new policy instruments are needed.

3. The policy could stimulate lending more directly than a base rate cut due to its direct impact on several benchmark lending rates.

4. The policy may have prevented recession and a descent into a deflationary spiral in Japan between 2001 and 2006.

**Arguments against quantitative easing**

1. A significant rise in the money supply always poses the risk of causing inflation.

2. Critics have argued that elements of the QE policy are a sign that the Bank of England has become blurred in their objectives. Many argue that an unstated goal of QE is to help the ailing financial system to recover from the financial crisis by injecting much needed liquidity, which should prevent financial institutions from collapsing and guard against risks posed from potential default by Eurozone governments. In addition, many claim another unstated goal of QE is to help the UK government borrow at reduced rates of interest, which is particularly important given the large size of the budget deficit since the 2008-9 recession. Finally, some argue that elements of the QE policy show that the Bank of England has become more focussed on boosting growth rather than controlling inflation. For example, the MPC announced the creation of a further £75bn to be injected into the economy in October 2011, at a time when inflation was well above target at 5.0%.

3. Since the asset purchase programme was extended beyond the initial £200bn in October 2010, the amount of liquid money on bank's balance sheets has risen by around 58% but loans issued to households and businesses has remained almost unchanged. This suggests that banks are holding onto this extra liquidity to improve their balance sheets, rather than increasing their lending, as the policy aimed to do. The fear is that when macroeconomic conditions improve and confidence returns, banks could increase lending significantly, thus increasing the effective money supply and inflation. However, the Bank of England could reverse the QE process and sell bonds back to the market if it looks like inflation may go above target.

*The Bank of England introduced quantitative easing in March 2009 and has now purchased £375bn worth of mainly government bonds to boost liquidity in the economy.*

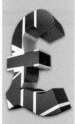

4. Towards the end of 2012 Mervyn King acknowledged that QE might be reaching the limit of its effectiveness. On 1st August 2012 the Treasury and the Bank of England launched the **Funding for Lending** bank scheme, where commercial banks can borrow from the Bank of England at low rates of interest (just 0.75%) on the condition that they increase lending to households and small businesses, with penalties if this was not achieved.

## Extension material: The relationship between money supply (M4) and inflation

M4 is a measure of the broad money supply in the economy and is often driven by bank lending. The general relationship between the money supply and the price level is a proportional one, as stated by the famous monetarist Milton Friedman when he stated that 'inflation is always and everywhere a monetary phenomenon'. The Fisher equation supports this view: MV = PT where M = money supply, V = velocity of circulation, P = price level and T = number of transactions or real output. If V and T remain constant, which is not unrealistic in the short run, a rise in the money supply should directly lead to a rise in the price level. However, V has varied considerably in recent years. Since 2008-9, low consumer and business confidence due to macroeconomic uncertainty caused agents to hold onto their money for longer as they are less willing to spend.

*Figure 9.3: M4 broad money and Nominal GDP*

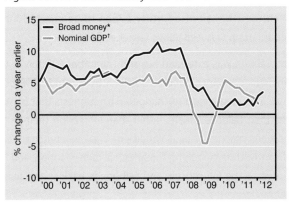

Source: Bank of England
*Excluding intermediate other financial corporations (OFCs) such as mortgage and housing credit corporations. †At current market prices, latest data Q1 2012.

If broad money growth exceeds nominal GDP growth (the rise in the value of output of goods and services) you would expect significant inflation to be the result. However, as shown in Figure 9.3 broad money growth was considerably higher than nominal GDP growth for much of 2000-2008, without causing significant inflation. There are a few possible explanations for this: money, especially consumer credit was being used to purchase large quantities of foreign goods; large quantities of money were being used to buy assets which caused high asset price (e.g. housing price) inflation but not wider inflation; broad money growth during this period was concentrated in the hands of OFCs (Other Financial Corporations) such as pension and private equity funds, which do not spend lots of money in the conventional sense; and lastly money may have been borrowed in the UK, adding to the money supply figures but spent on assets abroad.

There was a rapid fall in broad money growth from 2008 onwards, largely due to the Credit Crunch, where banks reduced lending considerably. The rapid fall in money supply growth in 2008-9 was a major cause of inflation falling below target by June 2009, and the threat of deflation became very real. This was a major justification for Quantitative Easing, which aimed to boost the money supply and reduce the risk of deflation. The £125bn of asset purchases made by the Bank of England in the nine months to June 2012 were a major factor in bringing about a rise in money supply growth in 2012. However, nominal GDP only rose by £30bn, providing more evidence that commercial banks were not passing on the money received from their sale of bonds to the Bank of England. This highlights the fact that the relationship between the money supply and inflation is far from straightforward.

## Questions

3. Explain how quantitative easing can be used to prevent deflation.
4. "The Bank of England has been very successful in controlling inflation since being given independence in 1997." To what extent do you agree with this statement?

# Chapter 10
# UK Fiscal Policy

In this chapter we explore recent changes to tax rates and trends in government expenditure under both the Labour and Coalition governments.

## ● Knowledge: Defining fiscal policy

Fiscal policy is government policy regarding taxation, government spending and borrowing. It is primarily a demand-management policy used to influence macroeconomic variables such as aggregate demand, but it can also be used to influence the supply side of the economy.

There are several objectives of fiscal policy:
1. To manage demand in the economy.
2. To fund government spending.
3. To correct market failures, such as the problem of public goods and externalities.
4. To redistribute income and wealth.
5. To improve the supply side performance of the economy.

## ● Knowledge: Types of taxation

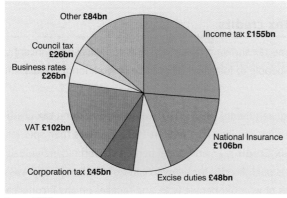

*Figure 10.1: Sources of government tax revenue 2012-13, £bn (OBR estimates)*

Source: HM Treasury

Total tax revenue for the 2012-13 financial year is expected to be £592bn. Business rates and Council Tax are collected by local authorities, but the majority of taxes are collected by HM Revenue and Customs.

**Direct taxes** are taxes levied directly on an individual or organisation, such as income tax, corporation tax or national insurance contributions (NICs). As shown by Figure 10.1, income tax is the most important contributor to government revenue, followed by NICs. Direct taxes tend to be **progressive**, where a higher proportion of income is paid in tax as the income level increases.

**Indirect taxes** are taxes levied on goods and services, effectively taxing expenditure. Figure 10.1 shows that Value Added Tax (VAT) is the most important source of indirect tax revenue. Other indirect taxes include excise duties, air passenger duty, customs duties and landfill tax. Unlike direct taxes, the burden of the tax can be passed onto a third party. VAT, for example, is levied on the producer, but they can choose to pass some of the burden of the tax onto the consumer. Indirect taxes tend to be **regressive**, where a higher proportion of income is paid in tax as the income level falls.

### Question

1. Identify two indirect taxes mentioned in the text that are part of Other Tax revenue of £84bn in Figure 10.1.

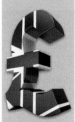

● Application: **Changes in UK tax rates**

*Table 10.1: Changes in UK income tax and VAT rates*

| Year | Income tax rates (%) | | | | VAT rate (%) |
| | Starting rate | Basic | Higher | New Top Rate | Standard rate |
|---|---|---|---|---|---|
| 1978 | | | | | 8 |
| 1979 | - | 33 | 83 | - | 15 |
| 1988 | - | 25 | 40 | - | |
| 1991 | | | | | 17.5 |
| 1992 | 25 | 25 | 40 | - | |
| 1997 | 20 | 24 | 40 | - | |
| 1999 | 10 | 22 | 40 | - | |
| 2008 | - | 20 | 40 | - | 15 |
| 2010 | - | 20 | 40 | 50 | 17.5 |
| 2011 | | | | | 20 |
| 2013 | - | 20 | 40 | 45 | 20 |

Table 10.1 shows a shift in the burden of taxation away from direct taxes such as income tax, towards higher indirect taxes such as VAT. Much of this shift occurred under the Conservative Government 1979-1997. Such a shift is controversial, as it made the tax system less progressive overall. This is partly responsible for the significant rise in the level of income inequality under the Conservatives as was explained in Chapter 4.

● Analysis: **Income tax and tax credits**

The reason for the cuts in income tax shown in Table 10.1 was to increase the incentive to work. Cuts in direct taxation encourage more people to join the labour force or work longer hours, thus boosting labour supply and supply-side growth.

A major initiative of the Labour government (1997-2010) was to vastly extend **tax credits** to poor working families, beginning with the Working Families Tax Credit in 1999. This was then split into two separate tax credits in 2003: the **Working Tax Credit** is an additional benefit to working individuals or families on low incomes. The **Child Tax Credit** is paid directly to the main carer of the family, and was designed to tackle child poverty. It is paid regardless of whether people work and families on any income can receive the Child Tax Credit, although high earning households will no longer be eligible from April 2013. The actual amount of child tax credits that a person may receive depends on these factors: the level of their income, the number of children they have, whether the children are receiving Disability Living Allowance and the education status of any children over 16.

Like cuts in income tax during the 1980s, the main aim of tax credits is to **make work pay**. This should reduce the unemployment trap, as the incentive to work is now greater. Many earners on low income face very high effective marginal tax rates, as earning more, perhaps through working longer hours will result in the withdrawal of certain benefits (e.g. housing benefit or free school meals) often combined with paying the 20% tax rate on the additional income earned. The Working Tax Credit, therefore, aims to boost the effective take-home income from work for low earners.

The abolition of the 10% starting rate of income tax in 2008 was widely criticised as many households on low income, and young childless single workers in particular, would see their disposable income reduced significantly, reducing the incentive to work. In the face of heavy criticism, the Labour Government expanded their tax credits programme to offset this. The Coalition adopted a key Liberal Democrat election pledge to raise the tax free allowance to £10,000 by the end of Parliament in 2015, thereby increasing the incentive to work and lifting millions out of income tax altogether. The tax free allowance had been raised from £6,475 in 2010-11 to £8,105 in 2012-13.

Chancellor Alastair Darling announced in the 2009 budget a new top rate of tax at 50% of income above £150,000 which came into effect in April 2010. The Treasury believed it would raise an extra £2.5bn per year. The arguments in favour of the new tax rate include:

- It would help to reduce the size of the large budget deficit.

- It could help to redistribute income.

- The income could be used to invest in public services.

- A populist view coming out of the financial crisis and the subsequent recession was that high earners created the economic problems but were not suffering to the same extent as those on low incomes or those made unemployed, and thus the new top rate was fair, showing that 'we're all in it together'.

Arguments against include:

- Individuals affected may reduce their spending due to a decline in disposable income, with adverse effects on employment and other tax revenues such as VAT.

- It creates a disincentive, reducing income earned and tax taken.

- International labour mobility has increased significantly over the last 20 years, particularly for high earners. Therefore, a 'brain drain' may occur as productive workers migrate to lower tax regimes.

- It may reduce inward foreign direct investment (FDI), and cause companies to move overseas, particularly in financial services where high pay is common.

- It may lead to significant tax avoidance through converting income into capital gains which is taxed at a much lower rate, or moving income to offshore tax havens, or bringing income forward (as was the case in 2009-10 before the rate came into effect).

A Treasury report published in March 2012 revealed that the 50% tax rate was probably yielding only £1bn per year or less, or even a negative yield. In the 2012 budget the Chancellor George Osborne announced a cut in the new top rate to 45%, effective from April 2013.

## Evaluation material: Income and substitution effects

If income taxes are cut this will increase the disposable income earned from every hour of work, which may entice the individual to work longer hours. This is known as the **substitution effect**, where the individual substitutes leisure time for work. The **income effect** works the other way. A worker might have a target level of post-tax annual income they wish to obtain, which can now be achieved by working fewer hours. Thus, the individual chooses to work less in favour of more leisure time.

Evidence suggests that which effect is greater depends on the individual, but some patterns within groups can be identified. Hours worked by females tend to be quite responsible to income tax cuts, while hours worked by males are almost entirely unresponsive. Both male and female participation rates are very responsive. Overall, direct tax cuts do increase the incentive to work.

## ● Analysis: **Corporation tax**

Both the Labour and Coalition governments have followed policies of significantly reducing tax rates. There are several reasons why such a policy has been pursued. The Exchequer have been keen to boost investment which is usually funded from post-tax profits, while continuing to attract large sums of inward FDI from overseas. Furthermore, lower corporation tax rates should encourage greater research and development, enterprise and innovation. All of this should boost long run economic growth. Government over the last 15 years have been keen to close the unfavourable **productivity gap** between the UK and some of her major competitors such as France and the US (see Chapter 6).

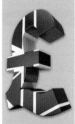

*Figure 10.2: International comparison of corporate tax rates, 2012 (%)*

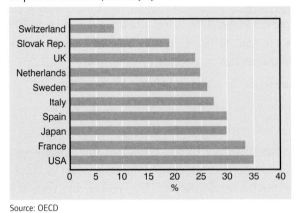

Source: OECD

The large company corporation tax rate was lowered from 33% to 30% between 1997 and 1999. In 2000 a 10% starting rate of corporation tax was introduced on profits up to £10,000, with marginal relief applying, meaning companies with profits of between £10,000 and £50,000 paid a rate between the 10% starting rate and the small companies' rate (19% in 2000). The 2007 budget saw the large company corporation tax rate fall to 28%, and the Coalition Government cut this rate to just 23% by April 2013. Crucially, the Labour government have introduced polices which reduced taxation paid on investment. As of 2001 small and medium sized firms were given a 40% capital allowance, and since 2008 most firms can claim a tax allowance on the first £50,000 of spending on plant machinery.

Figure 10.2 shows that the UK has a competitive rate of corporation tax relative to her main competitors, but the rate cuts in recent years has been necessary to maintain this position as other countries have also reduced their rates significantly.

## Extension material: Capital gains tax

The Labour Government in their early years of office were keen to show that they were 'pro business', and a favourable capital gains tax regime was set up alongside competitive rates of corporation tax. However, there was a perceived lack of fairness within the capital gains tax regime. Many individuals were subject to a 40% capital gains tax while wealthy executives from private equity companies only paid a 10% tax when selling a business, if they had owned it for at least 2 years. In the 2007 budget Chancellor Gordon Brown simplified the system by lowering the main rate from 40% to 18% and ensuring that private equity executives would pay this rate as well by abolishing the previous form of relief. However, many private equity executives still managed to pass off their effective income, known as a 'carry', as capital gains, thus subjecting themselves to an 18% tax rate rather than the much higher rates in the income tax system. As of June 2010, those who pay more than the basic rate of income tax were subject to a 28% capital gains tax.

## ● ● Knowledge and Application: Tax rises

*Figure 10.3: Taxes and national insurance contributions as a % of GDP*

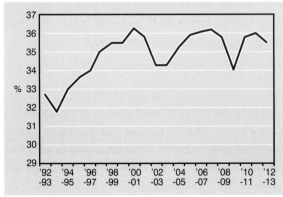

Source: HM Treasury

Despite cuts in income and corporation tax, many taxes have risen in recent years, including:

1. Under the Labour and Coalition governments, the threshold at which people start paying higher rates of income tax and NICs were not raised in line with inflation, and fell well behind earning growth. For example, between 2010-11 and 2011-12 the higher rate (40%) income tax threshold fell from £37,401 to £35,001. This has dragged more people into higher tax brackets, thus increasing their tax burden. This process is known as **fiscal drag**.

2. The rate of National Insurance paid by most employees, and most employers, has risen considerably since 1997. April 2003 saw a 1% increase in the standard rate of NIC contributions made by both employees and employers. The standard (class 1) employees contribution rate was raised by 1% again in April 2011, to 12%.

3. A number of new, indirect taxes have been introduced since 1992. Examples include the landfill tax, the climate change levy, the insurance premium tax and airport passenger duty.

4. There have been significant increases in council tax bills since 1997, which is a significant direct tax for most households. Council tax bills in England doubled between 1997 and 2010. Local authorities complained of under-funding from central government while being asked to increase their range of duties, leaving them no choice but to raise council tax bills and collect revenue from other sources such as parking charges. Following the 2010 election Local Government Secretary Eric Pickles put aside a £650m pot to support English councils willing to freeze council tax bills. All English councils took up the offer of support and froze bills in 2011, many continuing to freeze bills in 2012. Another controversy, however, is that **council tax is highly regressive**. It is paid based on outdated 1991 estimates of property values, and people in houses valued at £320,000 pay the same amount of council tax as those living in houses valued at £2m. Recent council tax rises have raised the tax burden disproportionately for those on low or fixed incomes.

5. As well as the introduction of a number of new taxes, since 1990 a number of indirect taxes have been increased in real terms, including air passenger duty, stamp duty, alcohol and tobacco taxes. In February 2007 air passenger duty was doubled. On the eve of the 2007 budget the Conservatives claimed that Gordon Brown had raised 99 taxes since he began at the Treasury in 1997. However, Chancellor Osborne cut fuel duty by 1p per litre in his 2011 budget, and delayed the planned increase in fuel duty responding to surging petrol and diesel prices.

## ● Analysis: **Increases in excise duties**

There are several economic justifications for raising excise duties:

- Demand for goods like alcohol, tobacco, and petrol is price inelastic. Therefore, a rise in tax will yield significant extra tax revenue for the government.
- Goods subject to excise duties are usually demerit goods which produce negative externalities, and are therefore over-consumed. Indirect taxation helps to correct this **market failure**.

Figure 10.3 shows that the UK tax burden has increased considerably since 1992. This was due to:

- The tax increases introduced by Chancellor Kenneth Clarke in the mid-1990s.
- New indirect taxes introduced by Chancellor Brown since 1997 as well as above inflation rises in indirect taxes.
- Higher rate income tax and NIC thresholds rising more slowly than inflation and earnings.
- Rising employment levels between 1994 and 2007 which boosted income tax and NIC receipts.
- Raising VAT to 20% in January 2011 boosted tax revenue considerably.

Figure 10.3 shows that tax and social security contribution receipts fell considerably due to the recessions of 2008-9 and 2011-12. The Coalition government, who have committed themselves to reducing the size of the budget deficit, have used a 20/80 rule of thumb; 20% of fiscal consolidation will come from tax rises, 80% will come from spending cuts. Given the size and persistence of the deficit, significant future tax cuts are very unlikely.

### Question

2. Why were the fiscal consolidation proportions of 20% tax rises and 80% spending cuts unlikely to be the reverse way around?

## ● ● Knowledge **and** Application: **Government spending**

*Figure 10.4: UK Government spending 2012-13 by area, £bn*

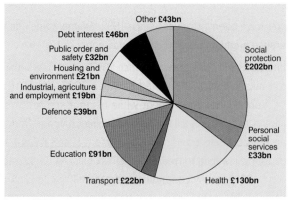

Source: HM Treasury

*Figure 10.5: UK government Total Managed Expenditure (TME), £bn*

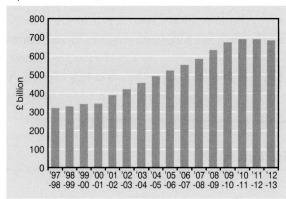

Source: HM Treasury

*Figure 10.6: TME as a % of GDP*

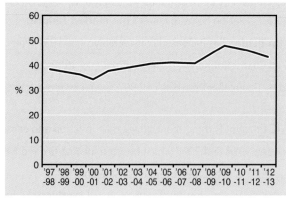

Source: HM Treasury

There are two types of government expenditure. **Current expenditure** is public sector spending on goods and services, such as medicines, and other types of recurring expenditure such as public sector salaries. **Capital expenditure** on the other hand, is investment in infrastructure such as motorways, railways, school and hospitals. Governments have been keen to boost capital spending since 1997, with major projects such as Cross-Rail, and the regeneration of the area surrounding the Olympic Park. The sum of these two types gives **Total Managed Expenditure (TME)**, which reached £683bn in 2012-13.

Figure 10.4 shows that the biggest single area of expenditure is Social Protection, which includes Jobseekers Allowance, Employment and Support Allowance, state pensions and other social security benefits.

## Analysis of government spending trends

The recession of the early 1990s caused the public finances to worsen significantly. The budget deficit reached 6.3% of GDP in 1993-4. The Labour government that came to power in 1997 pledged to be prudent in public expenditure, and avoid large budget deficits. In the first few years of office this objective was undoubtedly achieved. TME reached just 34.5% of GDP in 2000-1, compared to 43.0% in 1993-4.

From 2000 onwards, however, Labour increased public spending dramatically. Education, health, transport, housing, crime, and defence all received large increases in real terms expenditure. This spending boosted GDP growth significantly during the period, acting as a **Keynesian fiscal stimulus**. The 2002 Comprehensive Spending Review announced an annual average real increase in spending on health of 7.3%, and 5.7% on education, along with big boosts for other departments. Total expenditure on health rose from 7.0% of GDP in 2000 to 9.6% in 2010, finally surpassing the OECD average which the UK has lagged behind for decades.

However, the 2008-9 recession caused the budget deficit to increase dramatically, and despite the Coalition government's pledge to protect NHS spending, most government departments have experienced real terms cuts since 2010 as part of their fiscal consolidation strategy.

*Figure 10.7: Spending on healthcare and education as a % of GDP*

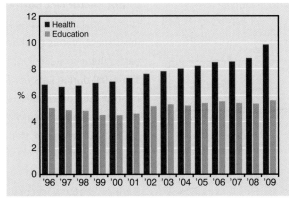

Source: OECD and World Bank

**How beneficial were Chancellor Brown's spending increases?**

There are several economic arguments supporting a rise in spending on the NHS. They are:

1. Rising life expectancy – The UK has an ageing population, who will require more medical care in their old age. Thus, more NHS spending is necessary to provide for their treatment.

2. Productivity and labour force participation – Better healthcare should reduce the number of people deemed to be unable to work due to health problems, thereby boosting participation rates and labour supply. Also, a healthier population should be more productive.

3. Increasing expectations – Higher standards of living has led to rising consumer expectations of the NHS.

4. Technological advance – As new and often expensive drugs and treatments have been discovered, people naturally want them. So new supply has created new demand.

5. The crisis in the NHS – By 1997 waiting lists for procedures were long and public spending on healthcare as a percentage of GDP was well below most of the UK's European neighbours.

There are several economic arguments supporting a rise in spending on education. They are:

1. Productivity and competitiveness – By improving attainment in education the workforce should become more productive, thus increasing supply side growth. As the UK has historically experienced an unfavourable productivity gap to her competitors, improving education is important. Furthermore, in a globalised world, the UK needs a skilled workforce to compete.

2. Social mobility – By 1997 many schools in depressed areas were underperforming and dubbed by the term 'sink schools'. By investing heavily in improving schools, particularly in poorer areas and through the academy program, greater equality of opportunity should result, thus improving social mobility, rising aspirations and a reduction in intergenerational poverty.

3. Plugging skills gaps – By the early 2000s there were skills shortages in many sectors which needed addressing.

## ● Evaluation: Have things improved?

With little doubt there has been a significant improvement in public sector healthcare and education provision since 2000, as well as improvements in other public services. Waiting lists are down, and educational attainment is up, spectacularly in some areas, such as London state schools. However, there is a serious question over how efficient public spending has been. A 2011 report by the ONS revealed that although public service labour input rose by around 15% between 2000 and 2008, labour productivity in the public sector actually fell during this period. In addition a measure of 'value added' public sector output growth lagged well behind the growth in public sector spending growth during this period, suggesting that higher funding was too often not translated into greater public service provision. A common criticism was that too much funding was used to hire administrative staff and managers, rather than on front line staff and services.

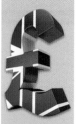

## ● ● Knowledge **and** Application: **Government borrowing**

*Figure 10.8: Public sector receipts, Total Managed Expenditure (TME) and Public Sector Net Borrowing (PSNB) as a % of GDP (excluding financial sector interventions)*

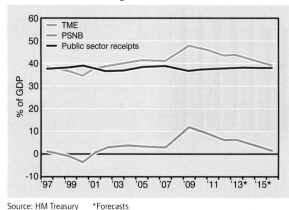

Source: HM Treasury    *Forecasts

*Figure 10.9: Cyclically adjusted Public Sector Net Borrowing (PSNB) as a % of GDP*

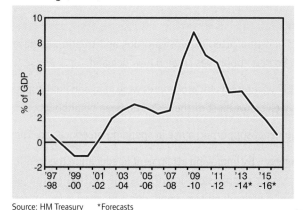

Source: HM Treasury    *Forecasts

**Public Sector Net Borrowing** (**PSNB**) is the sum of government current spending and net investment, minus total government revenue each financial year. Figures 10.8 and 10.9 show that during Labour's first term the public finances improved considerably. The government ran a budget surplus from 1998/9 to 2000/01, meaning that the PSNB was negative, and the government were able to reduce national debt levels significantly. During Labour's second and third terms however, the public finances worsened considerably. One of the biggest criticisms of Chancellor Brown was that he ran persistent budget deficits from 2001/02 to 2007/08, during a time of strong economic growth. This meant that a **structural deficit** was created as shown by the positive cyclically-adjusted PSNB measure in Figure 10.9. When the global financial crisis plunged the UK economy into recession in 2008/09, the government was already running a large budget deficit. Falling tax revenue and rises in welfare payments and discretionary spending caused public sector net borrowing to rise to 11.3% of GDP in 2009/10, leaving the UK with one of the highest budget deficits of all OECD countries. It should also be noted that Figures 10.8 and 10.9 exclude financial sector interventions, particularly the government's bank bail-outs in 2007 and 2008, which cost billions. The government may be able to get this money back when they sell shares in these banks back to the private sector, but the sale of some Northern Rock operations to Virgin Money at a lower share price than the government paid for them, and the current weak share price of RBS cast doubt on this view. Figures 10.8 and 10.9 show that even with the Coalition Government's planned fiscal consolidation, the OBR estimates that the budget deficit will not be eliminated until after 2016/17.

## ● Analysis: **Is the PSNB a problem?**

Budget deficits which lead to positive public sector net borrowing can be problematic for the following reasons:

1. National debt accumulation – net borrowing year after year leads to growing levels of national (also known as 'public') debt. Note the rising sector debt levels after 2007/8.

2. Rising interest payments on bonds sold – The government borrows issuing paper promises to repay a certain amount of borrowed money in the future, with interest. This is known as a bond. If the debt burden of a country appears to investors to be unsustainable, they will fear that there is a greater risk that they won't be repaid. Therefore, for the government to continue borrowing they may have to offer higher interest rates to sell bonds, which results in higher borrowing costs, and makes the debt even harder to repay. This is how the debts of Ireland, Greece and Portugal spiralled out of control in 2008-9, resulting in the need for bail-outs from the EU and IMF.

Figure 10.10: UK public sector debt as % of GDP (excluding financial sector interventions)

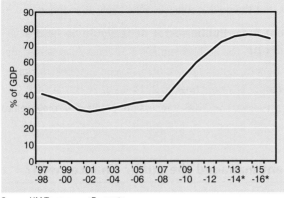

Source: HM Treasury    +Forecasts

3. Future tax rises and spending cuts – To reduce the rate of public debt accumulation, governments may have to raise taxes or cut spending in the future, which will reduce growth rates. This policy of 'austerity' has been widely implemented in EU countries since 2009.

4. Crowding-out – to borrow more, the government may have to raise interest rates on bonds issued, which may cause interest rates across the economy to rise. In turn, this may reduce private sector investment and spending.

5. Ricardian equivalence – if the government is running a budget deficit, consumers and firms will anticipate future tax rises and spending cuts. Expecting the resulting lower growth in the future they will save more and spend less. Therefore, the effects of expansionary fiscal policy may be partially offset by the compensating behaviour of households and firms.

A PSNB can be beneficial because:

● It can boost growth at a time when private sector demand is falling, providing a Keynesian fiscal stimulus. Governments around the world collectively ran a fiscal stimulus policy in 2008-9, which helped to prevent a 1930s style depression.

● If borrowing is used to boost capital spending (e.g. new schools, infrastructure), this can lead to productivity growth, thus raising the productive potential of the economy.

### ● Analysis: Why have the UK government's finances worsened since 2000/01?

● Lower tax revenues than expected in the mid 2000s.

● A deliberate large increase in spending on public services during Labour's second and third terms.

● Rising levels of unemployment after 2005 causing a rise in the welfare bill (e.g. more Jobseekers Allowance payments).

● The 2008-9 and 2010-11 recessions caused falling tax and N.I revenues, as well as a surge in welfare spending. Crucially lower tax revenues from company profits, especially due to financial sector losses. By 2007 10% of the Treasury's tax revenue came from 'The City' so financial sector losses reduced tax revenues significantly.

● Government rescues of banks like Northern Rock, Bradford and Bingley and RBS were very costly.

### ● ● Knowledge and Application: Labour's fiscal policy framework

The Labour government which took office in 1997 was keen to avoid the persistent budget deficits of the early to mid 1990s, and designed a new fiscal policy framework. The new framework was designed to be *transparent*, and bring *credibility* to fiscal policy, thereby bringing confidence to households and firms. The government set up two specific rules:

1. **The Golden Rule:** The government must only borrow to fund investment, not current spending. Therefore, **the government had to balance the current budget over the economic cycle**. Before the 2008-9 recession the Labour government claimed this rule had been met, but the Labour government only achieved this by changing the start and end dates of the economic cycle in the 2007 budget report, thereby 'moving the goal posts'.

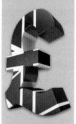

---

The unexpected severity of the 2008-9 recession led to an enormous increase in the budget deficit and borrowing, as shown in Figure 10.9. The government claimed that the fiscal rules had to be 'flexible' in these exceptional circumstances, but the golden rule was effectively abandoned.

2. **The Sustainable Investment Rule: Public sector debt would be held at a low and prudent level, not exceeding 40% of GDP.** The 2008-9 and 2011-12 recessions caused repeated large budget deficits to be run by the government, causing public debt to soar, as shown in Figure 10.10. In 2012 the OBR predicted that public sector debt would peak in 2014-15 at 76.3% of GDP. Given that growth has repeatedly fallen below forecasts since the 2008-9 recession, public debt may well exceed 80% of GDP by 2015.

## Evaluation: Has the government managed the public finances well?

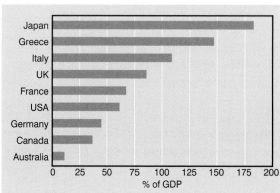

Figure 10.11: Total central government debt 2010, % of GDP

Source: HM Treasury

Figure 10.12: Selected European ten-year government bond yields

Source: Bank of England, *Inflation Report*, August 2012

During Labour's first term (1997-2001) they were fiscally prudent, and the public finances improved significantly, with public debt falling as shown in Figure 10.10. However after the 2000/01 fiscal year government spending rose considerably. Several taxes were raised and introduced but this was not sufficient to prevent the emergence of repeated structural budget deficits during a time of strong growth in the mid-2000s. Although the causes of the severe 2008-9 recession were arguably out of the government's control, going into that period running a structural budget deficit did not help, and the government's own fiscal rules had to be abandoned. Public debt rose to levels higher than in some other OECD countries as is shown in Figure 10.11.

When the Coalition Government took office in 2010 there were fears that investors could become alarmed by the rate at which UK public debt was rising, and that they would insist on higher rates of interest on government bonds issued. The Coalition government presented a detailed and strong commitment to deficit reduction, through tax rises and departmental spending cuts. Although Labour have criticised the government for cutting 'too far, too fast' and choking off the recovery, the policy has seemed to quell investor fears, as the UK government has been able to borrow at very low rates of interest, as shown in Figure 10.12. In part this has been due to investors fleeing from bond markets in struggling Eurozone economies such as Greece, Portugal, Italy and Spain, with bonds issued by the UK, Germany and the US being seen as relatively 'safe havens'.

## ● ● Application and Analysis: International comparison of public finances

The UK has usually been seen as a middle-to-low ranking country in terms of government spending as a proportion of GDP, embracing free markets more than many of her European neighbours. However, Figure 10.13 shows that government spending as a percentage of GDP in the UK was raised significantly between 2000 and 2009, causing the UK to move from below to well above the OECD average. This provides further evidence of the Labour government's more interventionist approach. However, government spending remains considerably lower than countries with a strong social democratic tradition, particularly in Scandinavia. The Coalition's deficit reduction policy is set to reverse the trend seen under Labour, as significant public sector job and spending cuts, combined with a robust rise in private sector output and employment is set to continue reducing the public sector's share of GDP.

*Figure 10.13: General government expenditures as a percentage of GDP (2000, 2007 and 2009)*

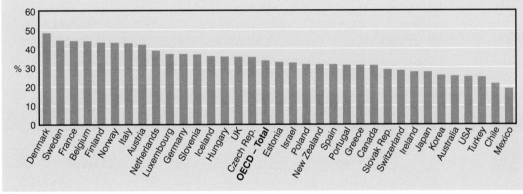

Source: OECD

*Figure 10.14: Total tax revenue as a % of GDP by country, 2011*

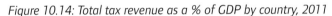

Source: OECD

Figure 10.14 shows that the UK is a middle ranking country in terms of tax revenues, with tax receipts as a percentage of GDP slightly above the OECD average in 2011. The UK has a higher tax burden than more free market economies such as the United States, but a lower tax burden than more interventionist North European countries. However, the introduction of the 50p tax rate gave the UK the highest top statutory rate of personal income tax in the G20. Even after the cut to 45p per pound, the UK will still have one of the highest top tax rates.

## ● ● Knowledge and Application: The impact of the Euro on fiscal policy

The EU Growth and Stability Pact (GSP), adopted in 1997 stated that countries joining the euro could not run budget deficits exceeding 3% of GDP, and national debt could not rise above 60% of GDP. Although the UK did not join the euro, Labour's fiscal rules followed a similar theme to those adopted by Eurozone countries, which aimed to stop Eurozone government undermining monetary policy by adopting contrary fiscal policy measures. France and Germany were the first ones to break the GSP. Following this, many Eurozone countries broke the GSP, and on the eve of the global financial crisis in 2007 many Southern Eurozone countries like Italy, Greece and Portugal had accumulated national debt levels around 100% of GDP. The global recession of 2008-9 led to a significant worsening in the public finances in most Eurozone countries and the GSP was effectively abandoned, like Labour's fiscal rules. By 2012 Eurozone countries were trying to carve out a new GSP, with harsher penalties for countries who break the rules, to ensure the Euro debt crisis is not repeated.

## Chapter 11

# The United Kingdom and Europe

This chapter will address the following key questions regarding the UK and Europe in 2013:

- What advantages and disadvantages arise from UK membership of the EU?

- What costs and benefits have arisen from EU enlargement?

- What advantages and disadvantages might arise from the UK entering into European Monetary Union (EMU) and replacing sterling with the euro as its currency?

- Given the economic crises in Europe since 2008, what might the future hold for the EU and the eurozone?

## ● Knowledge: **The European Union and the Eurozone**

The United Kingdom is one of the 27 members of the European Union. Table 11.1 shows how the European Union has evolved, from its initial existence as just a free trade area for coal and steel towards deeper and wider economic, social, political and even monetary union.

*Table 11.1: EU and eurozone members (as of January 2013)*

| Year joined EU* | Country | Currency = euro | Year joined EU* | Country | Currency = euro |
|---|---|---|---|---|---|
| 1952 | France | * | 2004 | Cyprus | * |
| | Germany | * | | Czech Republic | |
| | Italy | * | | Estonia | * |
| | Belgium | * | | Hungary | |
| | Netherlands | * | | Latvia | |
| | Luxembourg | * | | Lithuania | |
| 1973 | Denmark | | | Malta | * |
| | Ireland | * | | Poland | |
| | United Kingdom | | | Slovakia | * |
| 1981 | Greece | * | | Slovenia | * |
| 1986 | Portugal | * | 2007 | Bulgaria | |
| | Spain | * | | Romania | |
| 1995 | Austria | * | 2013 | Croatia (entry pending) | |
| | Finland | * | | | |
| | Sweden | | | | |

*or equivalent at date of entry

## ● Analysis: **What are the advantages of UK membership of the EU?**

The European Union is a **customs union** with free trade between members (freedom of trade in goods and services, freedom of movement of labour and capital) and common external tariffs imposed on imports from outside the EU; every member must set the same tariff (import tax) on imports of agreed goods and services.

The key microeconomic advantages of the **Single European Market** (**SEM**) are:

- EU members can specialise their production to create and deepen mutual gains from trade.

- The SEM creates European-wide competition, which should drive down costs of production, leading to…
  - Greater efficiency in EU firms
  - Opportunities for successful firms to enjoy economies of scale across Europe-wide markets
  - Lower prices and more choice for EU consumers
  - Greater incentives to invest, leading to dynamic efficiency gains

The key macroeconomic advantages of the SEM are:

- Productivity is raised due to increased efficiency and investment.

- Inflationary pressures are reduced across EU markets.

- Unemployment may fall as real wages rise and free movement of workers eases local labour market problems.

- GDP growth is encouraged.

The UK's Department of Business, Innovation and Skills estimate that EU members trade twice as much with each other as a result of the SEM. Over half of the UK's exports are sold to other EU countries. A European Commission study of the SEM in 2007 found that the SEM raised EU GDP by €233bn, adding 2.2% to GDP, and that 2.75 million jobs were created between the introduction of the single market in 1992 and 2006.

## Analysis: What are the disadvantages of UK membership of the EU?

Critics of UK membership of the EU (including the supporters of the United Kingdom Independence Party, or UKIP) point out the following issues with EU membership:

- Local and domestic unemployment resulting from UK firms either moving overseas or being competed out of existence by lower cost producers in the EU.

- Freedom of movement of labour has created competition in labour markets in countries such as the UK, where net migration has been inward.

- Increased immigration places pressure on public services, housing and infrastructure, particularly in regions where net immigration is particularly high.

- EU membership costs the UK over £6 bn per year.

- A significant portion of the EU budget is spent on the Common Agricultural Policy, which critics argue is inefficient, raises food prices, creates significant food waste and disproportionately benefits major agricultural producing members of the EU.

- As several EU countries have struggled to recover from the credit crisis and the recession which followed, there has been pressure on other EU members to contribute to 'bail-out' funds.

- Trade with other EU members has simply replaced trade which the UK used to conduct with other non-EU economies. **Trade creation** occurs when joining a customs union reduces the price of imported goods. **Trade diversion** occurs when joining a customs union increases the price of imported goods. In the latter case, it could be argued that when the UK joined the EU they were forced to buy more agricultural produce from within Europe, as the newly-imposed common external tariff priced non-EU trading partners such as Australia and New Zealand out of UK markets.

## Knowledge: EU enlargement in practice

The EU has grown from its original six members in 1952 and now forms an economic superpower with a population of over 500 million and a combined GDP of around £11 trillion (larger than the USA and Japan combined).

New members of the EU have to meet three following membership criteria:

- Political: viable institutions which support democracy, human rights and the rule of law.

- Economic: a market economy capable of competing within the SEM.

- Legal: acceptance of EU law (which takes precedence over domestic law) and a willingness to move towards monetary union when appropriate.

Croatia is expected to join the EU in 2013. Five other countries have been granted official candidate status, and these are Iceland, Montenegro, Serbia, Turkey and the former Yugoslav Republic of Macedonia.

## ● Analysis: **What are the implications of an enlarged EU for existing members such as the UK?**

In theory an enlarged EU will enhance the advantages of the SEM given new markets for UK goods in rapidly growing and developing markets. Access to cheaper raw materials and new sources of labour in new member states should also assist economic growth.

However the particular nature of many new members of the EU in recent years (and the future) has raised several concerns:

- New members tend to have lower GDP per capita than the average of existing members, limiting the potential for higher exports and profits for firms in existing states.

- New entrants are likely to be net beneficiaries from the EU budget (particularly if they have relatively large agricultural sectors), putting added pressure on the budget and potentially increasing pressure on existing members to contribute more.

- Workers in new member states may be more likely to emigrate as a result of EU enlargement, increasing immigration into higher income countries.

On this final point, it is worth noting that EU members can restrict immigrants from new members to some extent, and also migrants may be deterred from Western European economies where unemployment remains high after several years of economic decline and stagnation.

Immigration and macroeconomic performance is an important relationship to explore further. Critics of open immigration usually assume that migrants 'steal jobs' or claim benefits unfairly, placing pressure on public finances and public services. However, the eligibility of immigrants for domestic benefits, even when arriving from inside the EU, is not guaranteed and migrant workers can bring several advantages, such as:

- Filling skills gaps in domestic labour markets.

- Higher productivity levels and a stronger work ethic.

- Official economic migrants will pay taxes and make national insurance contributions, boosting the budget position.

- An increased supply of labour can keep wages lower, reducing firms' costs and dampening price inflation pressures.

A study by the Home Office in 2007 suggested that migrant workers to the UK had added £6 billion to UK GDP (creating a net macroeconomic benefit), but at the cost of added strains on public services and housing (thus creating microeconomic costs).

## ● ● Analysis **and Evaluation: The advantages of European Monetary Union**

The creation of the single European currency unit was until relatively recently seen as a major economic success story.

The UK's relationship with the euro has been mixed. In 1992, sterling was forced out of the Exchange Rate Mechanism, a system designed to calibrate and align Western European economies in preparation for the replacement of their own currencies with the euro, or single currency.

The Labour governments of 1997-2010 believed the UK could replace sterling with the euro, but only at a time and under certain conditions which would have benefited both the UK and existing member states.

The arguments given in favour of adopting the euro are:

- The elimination of **transaction costs**, or costs of exchanging currencies, when engaging in trade with other eurozone members.

- The removal of **exchange rate uncertainty**, encouraging greater trade and cross-border investment.

- Greater **price transparency**, as the calculations needed to compare prices in different currencies would no longer be necessary.

In effect, a single currency deepens the advantages of a single market to reinforce and extend the gains from trade, both in static terms (at a point in time) and dynamically (over time). However, there are drawbacks and dangers resulting from the adoption of a single currency:

- Menu costs: these are the one-off costs associated with changing prices, financial and commercial equipment, and even the notes and coins themselves.

- Inflation resulting from imperfect information: some economists argue that when a currency changes (for example during decimalisation in the UK in 1971), firms take advantage of consumer uncertainty to increase prices.

- **Loss of economic sovereignty**: this is most obviously the main drawback of joining the eurozone for an economy such as the UK. Since each currency can only have a single interest rate, the responsibility for setting interest rates in the UK would pass from the Bank of England to the European Central Bank. In addition, currency depreciation or devaluation against the euro (the currency of most of the UK's main trading partners) would no longer be an option, and thus the UK authorities would lose both monetary policy and exchange rate policy sovereignty, in other words two of their key policies for controlling the macroeconomy. Critics of the eurozone have also pointed out the difference between the UK inflation target and that of the European Central Bank, which sets the inflation target for eurozone members. The ECB aims to keep its equivalent of CPI inflation below 2% (compared with 2.5% + or − 1% for the Bank of England), which some economists see as dangerously close to the threat of deflation.

Whether the UK should adopt the euro or not depends to some extent on the following key factors:

- The exchange rate at which sterling is ultimately converted into euros. If this rate is too high, this will make UK goods and services uncompetitive against those of other eurozone members. Too low, and imports will be permanently expensive and the standard of living in the UK will suffer.

- The importance of policy sovereignty in the UK, which is closely linked to:

- The suitability of eurozone-wide policies to the UK economy.

This final point is closely linked to the concept of convergence. Chancellor Gordon Brown set out five 'convergence criteria' which he believed were necessary to determine whether the UK would benefit – and, indeed, survive – monetary union with the eurozone. Those criteria are:

1. Cyclical convergence: is the UK economic cycle aligned with that of the eurozone? If not, expansionary policies to boost an ailing eurozone could create excessive inflation in booming Britain; or conversely, European authorities would be using contractionary policies to limit growth in the eurozone at a time when the UK was facing recession and rising unemployment.

2. Flexibility: can the UK absorb and recover from exogenous (arising outside the domestic economy) and asymmetric (having unequal impacts) shocks?

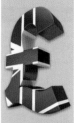

3. Inward investment: would adoption of the euro attract even greater investment from overseas?

4. Impact on the financial sector: would eurozone entry help or hinder the financial services sector in the UK, which is a key driver of growth and exports, and creator of jobs.

5. Impact on growth and employment: would the UK's adoption of the euro create output and jobs across the macroeconomy?

It is important to note that even over a period of 13 years under a government which had a strong faith in the desirability of adopting the euro for Britain, the decision was not made to go ahead with this policy. A comprehensive study was undertaken in 2003 which concluded that the UK would be ill-advised to enter into monetary union on nearly all these criteria.

The work of the economist Robert Mundell offers an interesting insight into the key characteristics of a single currency area. Mundell's theory of the **Optimal Currency Area** sets out the necessary conditions for successful monetary union. They are:

1. Labour mobility within the currency area.

2. Capital mobility and price and wage flexibility.

3. Economic cycle convergence.

4. Fiscal mechanisms to redistribute funds from higher income to lower income areas.

Taking each in turn, critics of the eurozone argue that a lack of a common language has hindered labour mobility. In addition, prices and wages are more flexible in some economies than others, mainly due to differentials in labour market policies and employee protection. In terms of economic cycles, the recent recession showed that some eurozone economies were able to recover more quickly from the crisis than others. It is interesting to note that the ability of sterling to depreciate against the euro and the dollar during the recession of 2008-09 gave a welcome boost to UK exports, albeit at the cost of higher inflation due to increase import prices. Such a gain – which some economists estimate reduced the severity of the recession by perhaps 1% of UK GDP – would not have been as likely had the UK been a member of the eurozone at this time.

The EU has resisted pressure from some of its supporters to introduce eurozone-wide tax levels. This would remove another lever of policy power from domestic governments, and arguably seriously constrain the only remaining option remaining, that of supply-side policy. Nonetheless, there are redistributive mechanisms in place, most notably Structural Funds (a form of regional policy, targeting EU money into poorer regions for investment in, for example, infrastructure projects) and the European Stability Mechanism (ESM). This leads on to the final section of this chapter.

● Application: **The UK and Europe – comparative data**

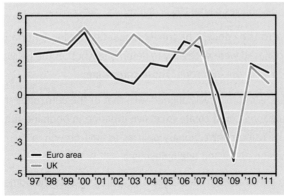

Figure 11.1: Real GDP growth in the UK and Euro area

Source: HM Treasury

This section compares UK macroeconomic performance with that of the eurozone (or, to use its official name, euro area) members.

The UK is closely linked – geographically and economically – to the performance of the rest of Europe, but Britain trades with non-EU members to a greater extent than other advanced Western European economies due to stronger historical and cultural links between the UK and North America, the Indian subcontinent and Oceania.

Figure 11.2: Unemployment in the UK and Euro area

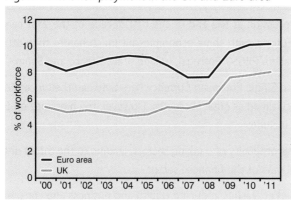

Source: HM Treasury

Figure 11.3: Inflation in the UK and Euro area

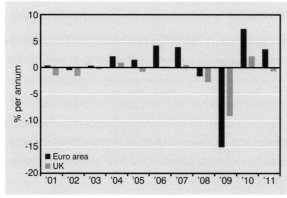

Source: HM Treasury

Figure 11.4: Growth of industrial output in the UK and Euro area

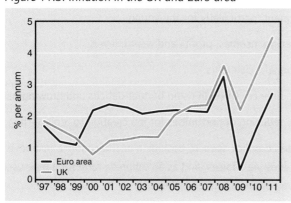

Source: HM Treasury

Figure 11.5: Productivity growth in the UK and Euro area

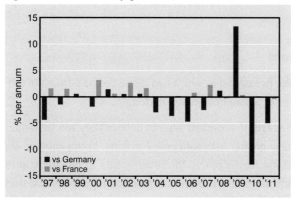

Source: HM Treasury

Over the course of 'the NICE decade', the UK enjoyed growth slightly above that of the eurozone average. Even when eurozone growth dipped in 2003, the UK enjoyed strong real growth, but during the recession of 2008-09 the UK and eurozone experienced very similar patterns of contraction.

Latest data from the end of 2012 suggests that the UK has recovered (albeit tentatively) from its recent double-dip recession, while the eurozone has re-entered recession (quarters 2 and 3 of 2012 showed contractions in GDP across the euro area, with even Germany and France recording growth of only 0.2% each).

The UK enjoyed lower unemployment and inflation between 2001 and the final years of 'the NICE decade', but since the recession in 2008-09 the UK has experienced higher inflation. This is most likely to have resulted from imported inflation due to weaker sterling.

The data given in Figure 11.4 shows the overall trend of deindustrialisation in the UK. Even during the strong growth of the NICE decade industrial output either fell or grew at very low levels (see 2004 and 2007). Industrial output rose at its highest rate in 2010 as the secondary sector bounced back from the dramatic fall in output in 2009.

The UK's productivity gap against other advanced European and North American economies was explored in greater detail in Chapter 6, and Figure 11.5 shows how the UK has typically underperformed in this area against Germany. Despite a boost in comparative productivity in 2009 (German industrial output fell by nearly 20%, with unemployment only rising 0.3%) the UK has seen productivity growth remain similar to that of France but considerably below German levels in 2010 and 2011.

## Question

1. With reference to Figures 11.2 to 11.5 how does the UK's macro-economic performance change during the period shown compared with the eurozone ?

## ● ● Knowledge and Application: Europe in crisis?

The credit crisis and ensuing recession at the end of the first decade of the 21st century carried major economic implications across Europe, with some economies hit much harder than others. The five most troubled countries are the so-called 'PIIGS': Portugal, Ireland, Italy, Greece and Spain.

The Single European Market and Single European Currency had, between their inception (1992 and 1999 respectively) and 2007, been acclaimed as great successes. However, the pressures on European countries have been very damaging, and include:

- Collapses in the liquidity and profitability of banking sectors, leading to the threat of bank collapses and the need for government bail outs of the financial sector.

- Housing market and stock market crashes, reducing wealth and business and consumer confidence.

- Business bankruptcies and falling profits.

- Rapidly increasing unemployment, particularly for the young.

- Falling tax revenues due to falling incomes, profits and wealth levels.

- Increases in unemployment benefit claimants.

- Resulting pressures on public finances through rising budget deficits and growing national debts.

- Stagnant or negative growth, reducing opportunities for job creation to replace the jobs lost.

The word 'austerity' has re-entered policy speech, both as a microeconomic response to low confidence and the need to make cheaper lifestyle choices, and as an umbrella term for a macroeconomic priority on closing the budget deficit above policies designed to boost growth.

The eurozone area has been forced to address the problem of growing diversity of incomes within its members. Structural Funds have been put under great pressure, both in terms of increased claims on the budget and the questioning of their value for money in the 'richer' economies which, until the recession, were willing and able to make net contributions in the cause of European integration.

In 2010, Europe's finance ministers approved a €750 billion fund called the **European Financial Stability Facility** (**EFSF**) to provide a rescue package for economies struggling to keep sovereign debt (national debt) under control.

Economies such as Germany and France have advocated conditions on these 'bail outs' to economies such as Greece and Spain. The key problem is that those economies hit hardest by the impact of recession have to make the deepest cuts in spending and increases in taxation to meet budget deficit targets, and these sharply contractionary policies can increase the speed of decline of GDP, leading to ever more severe automatic stabilisation (or fiscal drag) effects.

There are three main sources of funds (the 'troika') for troubled European economies:

- the European Central Bank

- the European Union

- the International Monetary Fund

As of November 2012, there were five countries which had requested help from the IMF and the European partners. They were Greece, Cyprus, Spain, Ireland and Portugal.

A key issue is that of **moral hazard**: if economic agents believe they will be helped during a time of difficulty, they may choose to take greater risks with policy-making. In this context, the provision of bail-out funds can be seen as reducing the incentive for governments of engaging in reform to make the necessary cuts in spending or increases in tax to reduce their budget deficits and thus bringing national debt under control.

## ● Evaluation: **How would a break-up of the eurozone affect the UK economy?**

Throughout 2012 the 'doomsday' scenario for the eurozone and the wider EU has been the potential for an economy such as Greece to leave the eurozone altogether, and reinstate their own national currency. The impact of such a 'Grexit' would have serious repercussions for the country leaving the eurozone. Economists have estimated that the living standards in such an economy might shrink by up to one third, and the price of imports would rise dramatically if the new currency was significantly weaker than the euro. As exports would be unlikely to make up the shortfall in domestic demand, the fall in aggregate demand would lead to increases in unemployment and even greater strain on the public finances. The possible likely impacts on the UK economy of one of the PIIGS economies leaving the eurozone and adopting a new currency would be:

● lower demand for UK exports in PIIGS

● a fall in the value of debt repayments, wages or revenues from economic agents in PIIGS

● large losses in the UK financial sector if banks are holding government or corporate bonds in PIIGS

● the possibility of default on government or corporate bonds from PIIGS

● reduced pressure on eurozone bail-out funds as fewer PIIGS continue to require support in the eurozone

● fall in foreign direct investment (FDI) from PIIGS into the UK

● the possibility of economic migrants from PIIGS seeking work in more stable European countries, such as the UK

● wider negative impacts on stock markets (and resulting falls in wealth)

● lower business and consumer confidence, increasing profit retention and saving and reducing the marginal propensities to invest and consume

● smaller (and possibly negative) accelerator and multiplier effects

● appreciation of the euro against the dollar and probably sterling (which is likely to be more dramatic if more than one of the PIIGS leaves the euro)

● this could stimulate the UK economy (similar to the export-led boom which followed from sterling leaving the Exchange Rate Mechanism in 1992) through improved price competitiveness and higher exports into what remains of the eurozone

The overall impact of one or more of the PIIGS leaving the eurozone will depend on:

● which country or countries leave the eurozone

● how many countries leave the eurozone

● the impact on business confidence and stock markets

● the impact on the euro-dollar and euro-sterling exchange rates

● whether PIIGS leaving the eurozone results in a wider loss of faith and confidence in European Monetary Union

Some economists have argued that the current crisis may lead to the rejection of the single European currency by even the stronger economies of Germany and France. The impact of such a breakdown would be dramatic, unprecedented and almost impossible to predict!

### Questions

2. Why might it be suggested that Germany would be better off outside the eurozone?

3. Why do some critics argue that austerity measures to meet budget deficit targets are self-defeating?

# Chapter 12

# The UK in the World Economy

This chapter examines the UK's position in the global economy, as well as the challenges and opportunities the UK economy is likely to face in the coming decades.

## ● Knowledge: **The UK and globalisation**

**Globalisation** is such a multi-faceted issue that it is hard to define precisely. Globalisation can be taken to mean the increasingly free flows of goods, services, capital, people, information and cultures around the world. Advocates of globalisation and free trade believe that countries will specialise in their area of **comparative advantage**. This is where one country can produce a good or service at a lower opportunity cost than another. Put simply, the theory implies that if each country specialises in producing the good or service they are relatively best at, resources will be allocated more efficiently, total global output should rise, and overall economic welfare will be improved. The so-called 'NICE decade' between 1997 and 2007 was a period of rapid globalisation.

## ● Analysis: **How has globalisation affected the UK economy?**

As shown in Figure 12.1, growth in global trade tends to rise more rapidly than world GDP growth, implying that imports and exports as a % of GDP have been rising in most countries, due to the increasingly free movement of goods and services. Figure 12.2 shows that between 1990 and 2012 global merchandise trade tripled, despite a fall in global trade during the 2008-9 global recession.

The UK economy is no exception, and has seen growing import and export volumes over the last two decades (see Chapter 5 for more detail). Imports and export values were equivalent to about 30% of GDP in 2012.

Figure 5.1 in Chapter 5 highlighted the UK's move to specialise in the production of services, in which it is a large net exporter, at the expense of manufactured goods exports, in which the UK is now an enormous net importer. Over the past two decades, the Newly Industrialised Countries (NICs) such as China and others in the Asian Pacific Rim have become able to produce manufactured goods at a much lower cost than producers in the UK and other Most Developed Countries (MDCs). At the same time the UK has a clear comparative advantage in the production of services due to the use of English as the international business language, a long standing reputation for excellence in professional services such as accounting, law

*Figure 12.1: Growth in volume of world merchandise trade and GDP, 2005-13*

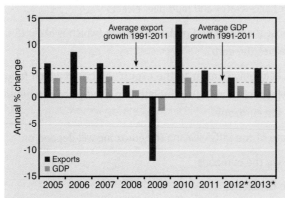

Source: WTO Secretariat    *Projected

*Figure 12.2: Volume of world merchandise exports, 1990-2013, Indices, 1990 = 100*

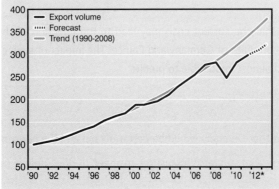

Source: WTO Secretariat    *Projections

*Figure 12.3: Manufacturing and financial services as a % of GDP*

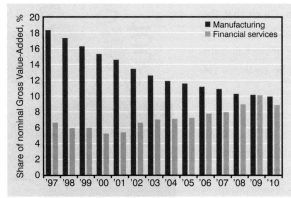

Source: ONS data from HM Treasury budget 2012

*Figure 12.4: GDP and financial services output growth*

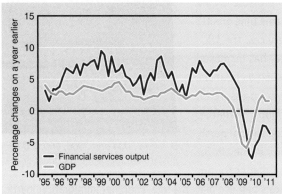

Source: Bank of England

*Figure 12.5: Share of nominal GDP accounted for by financial services*

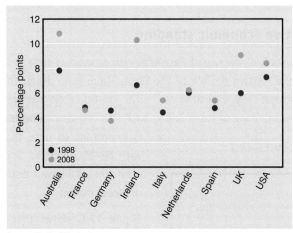

Source: Bank of England

and finance, and the existence of the City of London as the world's leading financial centre.

Figure 12.3 shows that the manufacturing sector has shrunk considerably as a proportion of the UK output since 1997, while financial services have grown in importance. According to the ONS business services and finance accounted for 29.3% of GDP in 2012, with manufacturing accounting for just 10.3%. Since the 1980s the UK's relatively more relaxed attitude towards free markets has led to governments doing less to support manufacturing in the face of new competition from East Asia than many of her competitors such as France and Germany, and significant deindustrialisation occurred. The manufacturing sector's share of UK GDP fell to levels significantly lower than France and Germany. Areas of Southern Scotland, South Wales and Northern England have been particularly affected by industrial decline. Some of these areas remain blighted by high rates of unemployment and welfare dependency. While manufacturing has declined as a share of GDP, Figure 12.4 shows that in the decade leading up to the 2008 financial crisis, GDP growth averaged 3% per annum while financial services output averaged around 6%, increasing the sector's share of GDP considerably.

Figure 12.5 shows that financial services' share of UK GDP has risen considerably between 1998 and 2008 to levels far higher than in similar-sized European economies such as France, Germany and Italy.

There are problems associated with being dependent on services and financial services in particular. Firstly services are more difficult to export than goods due to language barriers and regulation. The European Union, the destination for 50% of UK exports, has very effectively removed barriers to trade in goods, but has been much less successful in removing barriers to trade in services. Exporting services outside of the EU is even more difficult. The trade in services surplus is insufficient to outweigh the trade in goods deficit, leading to a persistent trade deficit. The second problem is that there are risks associated with being dependent on finance and banking. Unlike other sectors, if banks get into trouble and go bust there are much wider implications for the economy. Households and firms will lose their savings; other banks will become much less willing to lend and business and consumer confidence will plummet. In 2007-8 some of the UK's biggest banks such as RBS and HBOS faced bankruptcy. The Labour government decided that the

consequences of not bailing out these banking giants would be too great to risk, and spent billions of pounds saving them. Given that the share prices of the rescued banks have remained well below their level at the time of the bail-outs, it looks likely the bail-outs will be costly for UK taxpayers.

Globalisation has also had an impact on wage growth across different sectors, and has been blamed for rising wage inequality. Demand for low-skilled manufacturing products has declined, and the UK has a comparative disadvantage in this area. Less demand for basic manufactures means less demand for low-skilled manufacturing workers, thus putting downward pressure on the wages of these workers. At the same time greater demand for UK professional services, the UK's areas of comparative advantage, has increased demand for workers in sectors such as financial and legal services, putting upward pressure on wages in these already well paid jobs. Therefore, greater trade flows and specialisation partly explains widening wage inequality in the UK for much of the past 15 years (see Chapter 4), but

*Between 2004 and 2006, 600,000 people came from Eastern Europe to the UK, most of them from Poland.*

the increasingly free flow of workers has also played a role. High net immigration, particularly since the UK opened her borders to the 10 new EU member states in 2004 has increased the supply of relatively unskilled labour in the UK, thus putting downward pressure on wages in unskilled jobs. Between 2004 and 2006 600,000 people came from Eastern Europe to the UK, most of them from Poland.

● Knowledge: **The UK's relative economic standing**

Much has been made in recent years of the rise of East Asia, with economies such as China experiencing rapid economic growth, and the relative decline of the West. There is no doubt that the balance of economic power is changing dramatically, especially as the US and EU economies are still struggling to recover from the 2008-9 recession, many of them falling back into recession subsequently. However, it is important to note that the UK, along with North American and West European economies still have a disproportionate share of global income.

*Figure 12.6: Gross domestic product (GDP)*

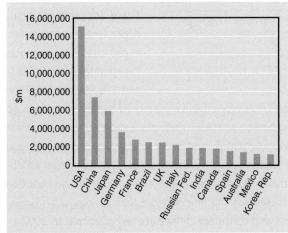

Source: World Bank

Figure 12.6 shows that the UK has the seventh largest economy in the world. The UK's share of world GDP is roughly 4%, despite having just under 1% of world population.

Despite high rates of GDP growth occurring in developing countries over the past 15 years, particularly those in East Asia, global wealth is still disproportionately concentrated in North America, Western Europe and Japan.

*Table 12.1: Merchandise and commercial services trade: leading exporters and importers, 2011, by rank and % of world total (merchandise trade, left-hand side; services, right-hand side)*

| Rank | Goods exporters | Share (%) | Goods importers | Share (%) | Rank | Goods exporters | Share (%) | Goods importers | Share (%) |
|------|-----------------|-----------|-----------------|-----------|------|-----------------|-----------|-----------------|-----------|
| 1 | China | 10.4 | USA | 12.3 | 1 | USA | 13.9 | USA | 10.1 |
| 2 | USA | 8.1 | China | 9.5 | 2 | UK | 6.6 | Germany | 7.3 |
| 3 | Germany | 8.1 | Germany | 6.8 | 3 | Germany | 6.1 | China | 6.1 |
| 4 | Japan | 4.5 | Japan | 4.6 | 4 | China | 4.4 | UK | 4.4 |
| 5 | Netherlands | 3.6 | France | 3.9 | 5 | France | 3.9 | Japan | 4.3 |
| 6 | France | 3.3 | UK | 3.5 | 6 | India | 3.6 | France | 3.6 |
| 7 | Rep. of Korea | 3.0 | Netherlands | 3.2 | 7 | Japan | 3.4 | India | 3.4 |
| 8 | Italy | 2.9 | Italy | 3.0 | 8 | Spain | 3.4 | Netherlands | 3.1 |
| 9 | Russia | 2.9 | Rep. of Korea | 2.9 | 9 | Netherlands | 3.1 | Italy | 3.0 |
| 10 | Belgium | 2.6 | Hong Kong | 2.8 | 10 | Singapore | 3.0 | Ireland | 2.9 |
| 11 | UK | 2.6 | Canada | 2.5 | 11 | Hong Kong | 2.9 | Singapore | 2.9 |
| 12 | Hong Kong | 2.5 | Belgium | 2.5 | 12 | Ireland | 2.6 | Canada | 2.6 |
| 13 | Italy | 2.6 | Rep. of Korea | 2.5 | 13 | Canada | 2.5 | India | 2.5 |
| 14 | Singapore | 2.2 | Singapore | 2.0 | 14 | Switzerland | 2.3 | Spain | 2.4 |
| 15 | Saudi Arabia | 2.0 | Spain | 2.0 | 15 | Rep. of Korea | 2.3 | Russia | 2.3 |

Source: WTO

Table 12.1 shows that as an open economy, the UK ranks highly in world share of imports and exports of goods and services. The fact that the UK is the world's second largest exporter of commercial services clearly demonstrates her comparative advantage in this area. In contrast, the UK is only the eleventh largest exporter of merchandise. The UK's relative economic position is forecast to decline in the years to come. Brazil's GDP eclipsed that of the UK in 2011, and India, Russia and Mexico are all forecast to have bigger economies than the UK by 2026.

## Extension material: Income convergence or divergence?

At the end of the Second World War, GDP per person in Western Europe was around half that of the US, and Japan's GDP per person was around one sixth. By 1990, income per person was roughly the same in these economies. Clearly convergence occurred between these economies. Income per person in Newly-Industrialised Countries (NICs) is rapidly catching up with levels in MDCs such as the UK, and some of the original Asian Tiger economies such as Hong Kong, Singapore and South Korea now have income levels comparable, or even higher, than most MDCs in the West. Global trade has grown enormously since 1945. The **Heckscher-Ohlin theory** states that with trade, capital intensive economies will tend to produce capital intensive goods as they can do so more efficiently than labour intensive economies, which will produce labour intensive products. Samuelson's **Factor Price Equalisation theory** states that if the cost of one factor of production (e.g. workers) is lower than another factor of production (e.g. capital) before trade takes place, it will rise relative to the other once trade takes place. Evidence from the US and China support this theory. The US has an abundance of capital compared to China, which has a relative abundance of labour. Since 1980, trade between the two countries has grown enormously. In China, wages have grown significantly. For example, unit labour costs in China rose by 9% in 2011, thus raising the cost of relatively abundant labour compared to relatively scarce capital. In the US, median real wage growth has stagnated since the late 1970s, thus lowering the cost of relatively scarce labour compared to the more abundant capital. The UK's experience has been very similar to that of the US, although median real income growth has been slightly higher. Although average income per person in China is around one tenth of average income in the UK, a process of *convergence* is clearly taking place. As wages in China rise, more capital is being used in the production process. In the US, as wages costs have been falling relative to the cost of capital, the US has experienced a 're-shoring' of manufacturing, as manufacturing domestically becomes more cost-effective than importing from China. However, this process has also occurred due to rising

transport costs, and technological advances allowing for the use of cheap shale gas in US production plants. However, income per capita in many of the Least Developed Countries (LDCs) such as Ethiopia and Myanmar has fallen behind incomes in MDCs, showing a *divergence* between the top and the bottom of the global income distribution. Several economic models, including the **Solow Growth model**, suggest that a certain amount of capital must be accumulated before an economy can '**take off**', and achieve self-perpetuating economic growth. To accumulate capital, economies must have reasonably high savings ratios, or bring in the capital from overseas, through trade or access to finance from institutions such as the World Bank. Many economies in Sub-Saharan Africa are unable to accumulate sufficient capital. Poverty leads to low savings rates, and primary product dependency leaves countries vulnerable to a worsening in the terms of trade, which means they can import less in exchange for their exports. In addition, some economists believe that LDCs must reach a certain 'social capacity' before they can take-off, through reducing problems such as corruption, and health issues to a critical level that allows for self-sustaining growth to take place.

## ● Analysis: How would 'rebalancing' help the UK economy?

### Switching from consumption and imports, to investment and exports

Since the financial crisis started in 2008, there has been a consensus amongst policymakers and economists that the UK economy had become too dependent on consumption (fuelled by excessive household borrowing) and imports. The Conservatives in particular also believe that the UK economy has become too dependent on government spending, funded by excessive borrowing. The Bank of England and the Coalition government have both called for a 'rebalancing' of the economy away from consumption and imports, towards investment and exports. This should help to bring more balanced and sustainable growth. A consensus has also emerged that the UK economy has become too dependent on services, and the manufacturing base of the economy has shrunk too much. Therefore many believe that boosting the manufacturing sector's share of the economy should be part of the rebalancing process.

Despite the consensus that rebalancing would be beneficial, there have been few specific policy initiatives designed to help the rebalancing of the UK economy. After a 24% depreciation in 2008, the pound has settled at a lower value that during 'the NICE decade' between 1997 and 2007. This should help to improve net exports, but the weaker pound was not the result of deliberate government policy. One government initiative to boost 'green' investment is the founding of the **UK Green Investment Bank** in 2012. The plc aims to attract private funds to finance the private sector's investments related to environmental improvements. The **Funding for Lending Scheme** (**FLS**), set up jointly by the Treasury and the Bank of England in 2012 aims to boost investment by enabling banks to borrow at lower rates on the condition that they lend more to businesses and consumers. One criticism of quantitative easing (QE) is that much of the cash injection has been stuck in the financial system, with banks remaining unwilling to lend, and many small businesses complain about the lack of access to credit, which impedes investment.

*Figure 12.7: OBR forecast change in shares of GDP 2011-16*

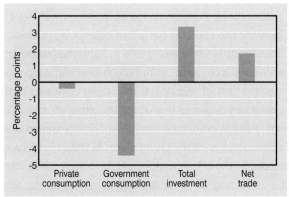

Source: OBR in HM Treasury budget 2012

The FLS aims to address this, by increasing the amount of loans given to businesses, and thus increase investment.

Figure 12.7 shows that the government expects the share of GDP accounted for by consumption and government spending to shrink, the latter by some 4.5%, and the contribution of investment and net trade to grow as a share of GDP between 2011 and 2016. The fall in government consumption's share of GDP is mostly due to the Coalition's spending cuts in an attempt to reduce the size of the budget deficit.

However, by 2012, there was little evidence to suggest that significant rebalancing had taken place, either in terms of the components of GDP in Figure 12.7, or between the manufacturing and service sectors. According to the ONS, since the Coalition took office in the second quarter of 2010, manufacturing accounted for 10.7% of GDP, and business services and finance accounted for 28.8%. By the second quarter of 2012, manufacturing's share of the UK economy had shrunk to 10.3% of GDP, while business services and finance had grown to 29.2%. Exports had risen from 30% to 31.1% of GDP over the same period, but net trade did not improve as the value of imports also rose, from 31.9% to 33% of GDP. In fact the UK achieved a record current account deficit of £20.8bn in Q2 of 2012. General government final consumption actually increased as a share of GDP during the first two years of the Coalition government's time in office from 22.9% to 23.5% while private sector investment's

*What can the UK do to boost net exports?*

share of GDP fell, and gross fixed capital remains 16% it's level in Q1 of 2008, before the economy entered recession. If the shares of GDP in the UK economy do rebalance, it is likely to take some time.

## ● Analysis: **What can the UK do to boost net exports?**

Many countries in the Eurozone have been gripped by an ongoing debt crisis and uncertainty over the future of the currency union since the world economy went into recession in 2009. As a result growth in Eurozone economies remains very weak, and in Q3 of 2012 the Eurozone went back into recession. Around 45% of the UK's exports go to Eurozone countries. Figure 12.8 shows that weak GDP growth in the Eurozone results in European consumers purchasing fewer imports, thus causing Eurozone import growth to remain very weak. This means there is little potential for a significant rise in demand for UK exports from Eurozone members.

*Figure 12.8: Real GDP growth and trade of euro area economics, 2008-11*

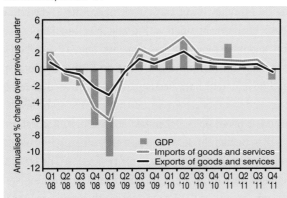

Source: OECD Quarterly national accounts

Faster-growing developing economies, on the other hand, provide a significant opportunity for export growth, and the Coalition government have been keen to boost trade relations with these economies. Since taking office in 2010 Prime Minister David Cameron has visited several of these countries on trade missions, including Brazil, China and the UAE. Germany has been very successful at growing exports, usually of hi-tech manufactures and capital goods, to the fast-growing developing economies such as the **BRIC**s (Brazil, Russia, India, China). German exports to China for example more than doubled between January 2007 and January 2012. The UK however, has so far been less successful at 're-orienting' trade towards these emerging markets, which is disappointing, but there is a clear opportunity for growth in this area. As well as trade deals, the stabilisation of the pound at below pre-financial crisis levels should help to make UK exports more competitive. Figure 12.9 shows that

the pound has fallen in value, while the currencies of China and Brazil have risen significantly which should help to boost UK exports to these emerging markets.

*Figure 12.9: Nominal dollar exchange rates, January 2005–February 2012*

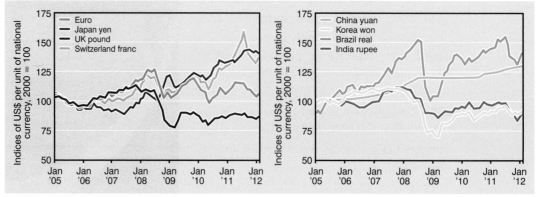

Source: WTO

*Figure 12.10: UK goods exports to EU and non-EU countries*

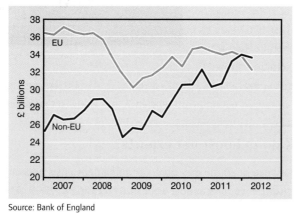

Source: Bank of England

Despite not being as successful in the re-orienting of trade towards emerging markets, UK exports to both India and China rose by around 55% in a 5 year period after January 2007, and Figure 12.10 shows that by 2012, for the first time in a very long time, UK goods exports to non-EU countries exceeded goods exports to EU countries. This is partly due to the fragile state of the EU economy, but it can partly be explained by higher exports to emerging economies.

## Outlook for the UK economy in 2013

The medium term outlook for the UK economy is not particularly optimistic. Growth forecasts by the OBR, Treasury and Bank of England have been downgraded with predictable regularity since the UK economy came out of the 2008-9 recession, and unemployment has remained above 2.5 million since 2009. For the UK economy to return to a sustainable growth footing it must go through several major adjustments. Households, many businesses and government have accumulated excessive levels of debt, and although deleveraging continues to restrict growth few would argue that current debt levels are acceptable or sustainable. In his Autumn Statement given on 5 December 2012 Chancellor Osborne said that it was harder to reduce borrowing levels than he had thought, and austerity measures would continue until 2018, rather than 2015 as initially planned when the Coalition took office in 2010. The UK is struggling to revive its manufacturing base, and remains very dependent on financial and business services, with all the associated risks. Rebalancing the components of GDP by increasing the importance of investment and net trade remains elusive. All the while problems in the Eurozone threaten to derail the UK's anaemic recovery and there is a real risk of a major external shock to the UK. A deep recession in the Eurozone, sovereign debt defaults by Eurozone governments or a breakup of the currency area could lead to plummeting UK exports, a banking crisis with a seizing up of credit, and a collapse in business and consumer confidence. Until households, companies and the government manage to reduce their debt levels, a lasting solution is found for the Eurozone crisis, and the UK successfully re-orients trade towards fast-growing emerging markets, strong and sustained growth is likely to remain elusive, and the UK's relative economic position within the global economy is set to decline.

# Index